SCHAUM'S *Easy* OUTLINES

BUSINESS

STATISTICS

D0846586

Other Books in Schaum's Easy Outlines Series Include:

Schaum's Easy Outline: Calculus
Schaum's Easy Outline: College Algebra
Schaum's Easy Outline: College Mathematics
Schaum's Easy Outline: Differential Equations
Schaum's Easy Outline: Discrete Mathematics
Schaum's Easy Outline: Elementary Algebra
Schaum's Easy Outline: Geometry
Schaum's Easy Outline: Linear Algebra
Schaum's Easy Outline: Mathematical Handbook
  of Formulas and Tables
Schaum's Easy Outline: Precalculus
Schaum's Easy Outline: Probability and Statistics
Schaum's Easy Outline: Statistics
Schaum's Easy Outline: Trigonometry
Schaum's Easy Outline: Principles of Accounting
Schaum's Easy Outline: Principles of Economics
Schaum's Easy Outline: Biology
Schaum's Easy Outline: Biochemistry
Schaum's Easy Outline: Molecular and Cell Biology
Schaum's Easy Outline: College Chemistry
Schaum's Easy Outline: Genetics
Schaum's Easy Outline: Human Anatomy
  and Physiology
Schaum's Easy Outline: Organic Chemistry
Schaum's Easy Outline: Applied Physics
Schaum's Easy Outline: Physics
Schaum's Easy Outline: Programming with C++
Schaum's Easy Outline: Programming with Java
Schaum's Easy Outline: Basic Electricity
Schaum's Easy Outline: Electromagnetics
Schaum's Easy Outline: Introduction to Psychology
Schaum's Easy Outline: French
Schaum's Easy Outline: German
Schaum's Easy Outline: Spanish
Schaum's Easy Outline: Writing and Grammar

SCHAUM'S *Easy* OUTLINES

BUSINESS STATISTICS

BASED ON SCHAUM'S
*Outline of Theory and Problems of
Business Statistics, Third Edition*
BY LEONARD J. KAZMIER, Ph.D.

ABRIDGEMENT EDITORS
DANIEL L. FULKS, Ph.D.
AND
MICHAEL K. STATON

SCHAUM'S OUTLINE SERIES
McGRAW-HILL

*New York   Chicago   San Francisco   Lisbon   London   Madrid
Mexico City   Milan   New Delhi   San Juan
Seoul   Singapore   Sydney   Toronto*

The *McGraw·Hill* Companies

LEONARD J. KAZMIER is Professor of Decision and Information Systems at Arizona State University. He received his bachelor's and master's degrees from Wayne State University and his Ph.D. from The Ohio State University. He previously taught at Wayne State and the University of Notre Dame. He is the author or coauthor of books on management concepts, statistical analysis, and computer applications in business. He is a charter member of the Decision Sciences Institute, in which he has held several national elective offices.

DANIEL L. FULKS is Associate Professor and Director of the Accounting Program at Transylvania University in Lexington, Kentucky. He received a B.S. from the University of Tennessee, an M.B.A. from the University of Maryland, and a Ph.D. from Georgia State University. He is also a Certified Public Accountant. He taught previously at the University of Kentucky and worked in private business for several years. He is the abridgement editor of *Schaum's Easy Outline: Principles of Accounting*.

MICHAEL K. STATON is an associate with the accounting firm KPMG LLP in Denver, Colorado. He received a B.A. in accounting from Transylvania University in Lexington, Kentucky, and an M.T. from the University of Denver.

3 4 5 6 7 8 9 0   DSH/DSH   0 1 0 9 8 7 6

ISBN 0-07-139876-7

Contents

v

SCHAUM'S *Easy* OUTLINES

BUSINESS
STATISTICS

Chapter 1
ANALYZING
BUSINESS DATA

IN THIS CHAPTER:

✔ *Definition of Business Statistics*
✔ *Descriptive and Inferential Statistics*
✔ *Types of Applications in Business*
✔ *Discrete and Continuous Variables*
✔ *Obtaining Data through Direct Observation vs. Surveys*
✔ *Methods of Random Sampling*
✔ *Other Sampling Methods*
✔ *Solved Problems*

Definition of Business Statistics

Statistics refers to the body of techniques used for collecting, organizing, analyzing, and interpreting data. The data may be quantitative, with values expressed numerically, or they may be qualitative, with characteristics such as consumer preferences being tabulated. Statistics are used in business to help make better decisions by understanding the sources of variation and by uncovering patterns and relationships in business data.

Descriptive and Inferential Statistics

Descriptive statistics include the techniques that are used to summarize and describe numerical data for the purpose of easier interpretation. These methods can either be graphical or involve computational analysis.

Inferential statistics include those techniques by which decisions about a statistical population or process are made based only on a sample having been observed. Because such decisions are made under conditions of uncertainty, the use of probability concepts is required. Whereas the measured characteristics of a sample are called *sample statistics*, the measured characteristics of a statistical population are called *population parameters*. The procedure by which the characteristics of all the members of a defined population are measured is called a *census*. When statistical inference is used in process control, the sampling is concerned particularly with uncovering and controlling the sources of variation in the quality of the output.

Types of Applications in Business

The methods of *classical statistics* were developed for the analysis of sample data, and for the purpose of inference about the population from which the sample was selected. There is explicit exclusion of personal judgments about the data, and there is an implicit assumption that sampling is done from a static population. The methods of *decision analysis* focus on incorporating managerial judgments into statistical analysis. The methods of *statistical process control* are used with the premise that the output of a process may not be stable. Rather, the process may be dynamic, with assignable causes associated with variation in the quality of the output over time.

Discrete and Continuous Variables

A *discrete variable* can have observed values only at isolated points along a scale of values. In business statistics, such data typically occur through the process of counting; hence, the values generally are expressed as integers. A *continuous variable* can assume a value at any fractional point along a specified interval of values.

You Need to Know

Continuous data are generated by the process of measuring.

Obtaining Data through Direct Observation vs. Surveys

One way data can be obtained is by direct observation. This is the basis for the actions that are taken in statistical process control, in which samples of output are systemically assessed. Another form of direct observation is a *statistical experiment*, in which there is overt control over some or all of the factors that may influence the variable being studied, so that possible causes can be identified.

In some situations it is not possible to collect data directly but, rather, the information has to be obtained from individual respondents. A *statistical survey* is the process of collecting data by asking individuals to provide the data. The data may be obtained through such methods as personal interviews, telephone interviews, or written questionnaires.

Methods of Random Sampling

Random sampling is a type of sampling in which every item in a population of interest, or target population, has a known, and usually equal, chance of being chosen for inclusion in the sample. Having such a sample ensures that the sample items are chosen without bias and provides the statistical basis for determining the confidence that can be associated with the inferences. A random sample is also called a *probability sample,* or *scientific sample.* The four principal methods of random sampling are the simple, systematic, stratified, and cluster sampling methods.

A *simple random sample* is one in which items are chosen individually from the target population on the basis of chance. Such chance selection is similar to the random drawing of numbers in a lottery. However, in statistical sampling a table of random numbers or a random number generator computer program generally is used to identify the numbered items in the population that are to be selected for the sample.

A *systematic sample* is a random sample in which the items are selected from the population at a uniform interval of a listed order, such as choosing every tenth account receivable for the sample. The first account of the ten accounts to be included in the sample would be chosen randomly (perhaps by reference to a table of random numbers). A particular concern with systematic sampling is the existence of any periodic, or cyclical, factor in the population listing that could lead to a systematic error in the sample results.

In *stratified sampling* the items in the population are first classified into separate subgroups, or strata, by the researcher on the basis of one or more important characteristics. Then a simple random or systematic sample is taken separately from each stratum. Such a sampling plan can be used to ensure proportionate representation of various population subgroups in the sample. Further, the required sample size to achieve a given level of precision typically is smaller than it is with random sampling, thereby reducing sampling cost.

Cluster sampling is a type of random sampling in which the population items occur naturally in subgroups. Entire subgroups, or clusters, are then randomly sampled.

Other Sampling Methods

Although a nonrandom sample can turn out to be representative of the population, there is difficulty in assuming beforehand that it will be unbiased, or in expressing statistically the confidence that can be associated with inferences from such a sample.

A *judgment sample* is one in which an individual selects the items to be included in the sample. The extent to which such a sample is representative of the population then depends on the judgment of that individual and cannot be statistically assessed.

A *convenience sample* includes the most easily accessible measurements, or observations, as is implied by the word convenience.

A *strict random sample* is not usually feasible in statistical process control, since only readily available items or transactions can easily be inspected. In order to capture changes that are taking place in the quality of process output, small samples are taken at regular intervals of time. Such a sampling scheme is called the *method of rational subgroups*. Such sample data are treated as if random samples were taken at each point in time, with the understanding that one should be alert to any known reasons why such a sampling scheme could lead to biased results.

Remember

The four principal methods of random sampling are the simple, systematic, stratified, and cluster sampling methods.

Solved Problems

Solved Problem 1.1 Indicate which of the following terms or operations are concerned with a sample or sampling (S), and which are concerned with a population (P): (a) group measures called parameters, (b) use of inferential statistics, (c) taking a census, (d) judging the quality of an incoming shipment of fruit by inspecting several crates of the large number included in the shipment.

Solution: (a) P, (b) S, (c) P, (d) S

Solved Problem 1.2 Indicate which of the following types of information could be used most readily in either classical statistical inference (CI), decision analysis (DA), or statistical process control (PC): (a) managerial judgments about the likely level of sales for a new product, (b) subjecting every fiftieth car assembled to a comprehensive quality evaluation, (c) survey results for a simple random sample of people who purchased a particular car model, (d) verification of bank account balances for a systematic random sample of accounts.

Solution: (a) DA, (b) PC, (c) CI, (d) CI

Solved Problem 1.3 For the following types of values, designate discrete variables (D) and continuous variables (C): (a) weight of the contents of a package of cereal, (b) diameter of a bearing, (c) number of defective items produced, (d) number of individuals in a geographic area who are collecting unemployment benefits, (e) the average number of prospective customers contacted per sales representative during the past month, (f) dollar amount of sales.

Solution: (a) C, (b) C, (c) D, (d) D, (e) C, (f) D

Solved Problem 1.4 Indicate which of the following data-gathering procedures would be considered an experiment (E), and which would be considered a survey (S): (a) a political poll of how individuals intend to vote in an upcoming election, (b) customers in a shopping mall interviewed about why they shop there, (c) comparing two approaches to marketing an annuity policy by having each approach used in comparable geographic areas.

Solution: (a) S, (b) S, (c) E

Solved Problem 1.5 Indicate which of the following types of samples best exemplify or would be concerned with either a judgment sample (J), a convenience sample (C), or the method of rational subgroups (R): (a) Samples of five light bulbs each are taken every 20 minutes in a production process to determine their resistance to high voltage, (b) a beverage company assesses consumer response to the taste of a proposed alcohol-free beer by taste tests in taverns located in the city where the corporate offices are located, (c) an opinion pollster working for a political candidate talks to people at various locations in the district based on the assessment that the individuals appear representative of the district's voters.

Solution: (a) R, (b) C, (c) J

Chapter 2
STATISTICAL PRESENTATIONS AND GRAPHICAL DISPLAYS

IN THIS CHAPTER:

- ✔ Frequency Distributions
- ✔ Class Intervals
- ✔ Histograms and Frequency Polygons
- ✔ Frequency Curves
- ✔ Cumulative Frequency Distributions
- ✔ Relative Frequency Distributions
- ✔ The "And-Under" Type of Frequency Distributions
- ✔ Stem-and-Leaf Diagrams
- ✔ Dotplots
- ✔ Pareto Charts

✔ *Bar Charts and Line Graphs*
✔ *Run Charts*
✔ *Pie Charts*
✔ *Solved Problems*

Frequency Distributions

A *frequency distribution* is a table in which possible values are grouped into classes, and the number of observed values which fall into each class is recorded. Data organized in a frequency distribution are called *grouped data*. In contrast, for *ungrouped data* every observed value of the random variable is listed.

Class Intervals

For each class in a frequency distribution, the lower and upper *stated class limits* indicate the values included within the class. In contrast, the *exact class limits*, or *class boundaries*, are the specific points that serve to separate adjoining classes along a measurement scale for continuous variables. Exact class limits can be determined by identifying the points that are halfway between the upper and lower stated class limits, respectively, of adjoining classes.

The *class interval* identifies the range of values included within a class and can be determined by subtracting the lower exact class limit from the upper exact class limit for the class. When exact limits are not identified, the class interval can be determined by subtracting the lower stated limit for a class from the lower stated limit of the adjoining next-higher class. Finally, for certain purposes the values in a class often are represented by the *class midpoint*, which can be determined by adding one half of the class interval to the lower exact limit of the class.

For data that are distributed in a highly nonuniform way, such as annual salary data for a variety of occupations, *unequal class intervals* may be desirable. In such a case, the larger class intervals are used for the ranges of values in which there are relatively few observations.

Note!

It is generally desirable that all class intervals in a given frequency distribution be equal. A formula to determine the approximate class interval to be used is:
Approximate interval =
(Largest value in data – Smallest value in data)
Number of classes desired

Histograms and Frequency Polygons

A *histogram* is a bar graph of a frequency distribution. Typically, the exact class limits are entered along the horizontal axis of the graph while the numbers of observations are listed along the vertical axis. However, class midpoints instead of class limits also are used to identify the classes.

A *frequency polygon* is a line graph of a frequency distribution. The two axes are similar to those of the histogram except that the midpoint of each class typically is identified along the horizontal axis. The number of observations in each class is represented by a dot above the midpoint of the class, and these dots are joined by a series of line segments to form a polygon.

Frequency Curves

A frequency curve is a smoothed frequency polygon.
In terms of skewness, a frequency curve can be:
1. *negatively skewed*: nonsymmetrical with the "tail" to the left;
2. *positively skewed*: nonsymmetrical with the "tail" to the right; or
3. *symmetrical*.
In terms of kurtosis, a frequency curve can be:
1. *platykurtic*: flat, with the observations distributed relatively evenly across the classes;

2. *leptokurtic*: peaked, with the observations concentrated within a narrow range of values; or

3. *mesokurtic*: neither flat nor peaked, in terms of the distribution of observed values.

Cumulative Frequency Distributions

A *cumulative frequency distribution* identifies the cumulative number of observations included below the upper exact limit of each class in the distribution. The cumulative frequency for a class can be determined by adding the observed frequency for that class to the cumulative frequency for the preceding class.

The graph of a cumulative frequency distribution is called an *ogive*. For the less-than type of cumulative distribution, this graph indicates the cumulative frequency below each exact class limit of the frequency distribution. When such a line graph is smoothed, it is called an *ogive curve*.

Remember

Terms of skewness: Negatively skewed, Positively skewed, or Symmetrical.
Terms of kurtosis: Platykurtic, Leptokurtic, or Mesokurtic.

Relative Frequency Distributions

A *relative frequency distribution* is one in which the number of observations associated with each class has been converted into a relative frequency by dividing by the total number of observations in the entire distribution. Each relative frequency is thus a proportion, and can be converted into a percentage by multiplying by 100.

One of the advantages associated with preparing a relative frequency distribution is that the cumulative distribution and the ogive for such a distribution indicate the cumulative proportion of observations up to the various possible values of the variable. A *percentile* value is the cumulative percentage of observations up to a designated value of a variable.

The "And-Under" Type of Frequency Distribution

The class limits that are given in computer-generated frequency distributions usually are "and-under" types of limits. For such limits, the stated class limits are also the exact limits that define the class. The values that are grouped in any one class are equal to or greater than the lower class limit, and up to but not including the value of the upper class limit. A descriptive way of presenting such class limits is :

5 and under 8   8 and under 11

In addition to this type of distribution being more convenient to implement for computer software, it sometimes also reflects a more "natural" way of collecting the data in the first place. For instance, people's ages generally are reported as the age at the last birthday, rather than the age at the nearest birthday. Thus, to be 24 years old is to be at least 24 but less than 25 years old.

Stem-and-Leaf Diagrams

A *stem-and-leaf diagram* is a relatively simple way of organizing and presenting measurements in a rank-ordered bar chart format. This is a popular technique in *exploratory data analysis*. As the name implies, exploratory data analysis is concerned with techniques for preliminary analyses of data in order to gain insights about patterns and relationships. Frequency distributions and the associated graphic techniques covered in the previous sections of this chapter are also often used for this purpose. In contrast, *confirmatory data analysis* includes the principal methods of statistical inference that constitute most of this book. Confirmatory data analysis is concerned with coming to final statistical conclusions about patterns and relationships in data.

A stem-and-leaf diagram is similar to a histogram, except that it is easier to construct and shows the actual data values, rather than having the specific values lost by being grouped into defined classes. However, the technique is most readily applicable and meaningful only if the first

digit of the measurement, or possibly the first two
digits, provides a good basis for separating data into
groups, as in test scores. Each group then is analogous to a class or category in a frequency distribution.
Where the first digit alone is used to group the measurements, the name stem-and-leaf refers to the fact that the first digit is
the stem, and each of the measurements with that first-digit value becomes a leaf in the display.

Dotplots

A *dotplot* is similar to a histogram in that a distribution of the data value
is portrayed graphically. However, the difference is that the values are
plotted *individually*, rather than being grouped into classes. Dotplots are
more applicable for small data sets, for which grouping the values into
classes of a frequency distribution is not warranted. Dotplots are particularly useful for comparing two different data sets, or two subgroups of
a data set.

Pareto Charts

A *Pareto chart* is similar to a histogram, except that it is a frequency bar
chart for a *qualitative variable*, rather than being used for quantitative
data that have been grouped into classes. The bars of the chart, which can
represent either frequencies or relative frequencies, are arranged in descending order from left to right. This arrangement results in the most important categories of data, according to frequency of occurrence, being
located at the initial positions in the chart. Pareto charts are used in
process control to tabulate the causes associated with assignable-cause
variations in the quality of process output. It is typical that only a few categories of causes are associated with most quality problems, and Pareto
charts permit worker teams and managers to focus on these most important areas that are in need of corrective action.

Bar Charts and Line Graphs

A *time series* is a set of observed values, such as production or sales data,
for a sequentially ordered series of time periods. For the purpose of

graphic presentation, both bar charts and line graphs are useful. A *bar chart* depicts the time-series amounts by a series of bars. A *component bar chart* portrays subdivisions within the bars on the chart. A *line graph* portrays time-series amounts by a connected series of line segments.

Run Charts

A *run chart* is a plot of data values in the time-sequence order in which they were observed. The values that are plotted can be the individual observed values or summary values, such as a series of sample means. When lower and upper limits for acceptance sampling are added to such a chart, it is called a *control chart*.

Pie Charts

A *pie chart* is a pie-shaped figure in which the pieces of the pie represent divisions of a total amount, such as the distribution of a company's sales dollar. A *percentage pie chart* is one in which the values have been converted into percentages in order to make them easier to compare.

Solved Problems

Solved Problem 2.1

Rental rate	Number of apartments
$350–379	3
380–409	8
410–439	10
440–469	13
470–499	33
500–529	40
530–559	35
560–589	30
590–619	16
620–649	12
Total	200

**Table 2-1 Frequency distribution of
monthly apartment rental rates for 200
studio apartments**

(a) What are the lower and upper stated limits of the first class?
(b) What are the lower and upper exact limits of the first class?
(c) The class interval used is the same for all classes of the distribution. What is the interval size?
(d) What is the midpoint of the first class?
(e) What are the lower and upper exact limits of the class in which the largest number of apartment rental rates was tabulated?
(f) Suppose a monthly rental rate of $439.50 were reported. Identify the lower and upper stated limits of the class in which this observation would be tallied.

Solution

(a) $350 and $379
(b) $340.50 and $379.50
(c) Focus on the interval of values in the first class.
$379.50 − $349.50 = $30
(d) $349.50 + 30/2 = $349.50 + $15.00 = $364.50
(e) $499.50 and $529.50
(f) $440 and $469

Solved Problem 2.2 Prepare a histogram for the data in Table 2.1

Solution

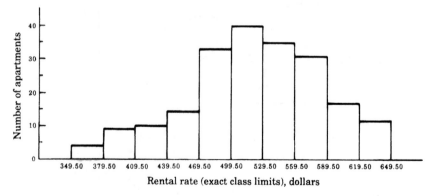

Rental rate (exact class limits), dollars

Figure 2-1

Solved Problem 2.3 Prepare a frequency polygon and a frequency curve for the data in Table 2.1. Describe the frequency curve from the standpoint of skewness.

Solution

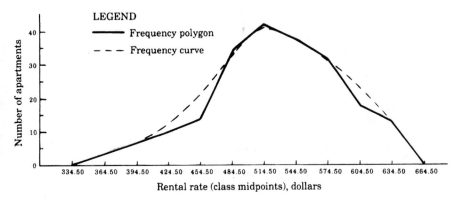

Figure 2-2

The frequency curve appears to be somewhat negatively skewed.

Solved Problem 2.4 Prepare a cumulative frequency distribution for Table 2.1. Present the cumulative frequency distribution graphically by means of an ogive curve.

Solution

Rental rate	Class boundaries	Number of apartments	Cumulative frequency (cf)
$350–379	$349.50–379.50	3	3
380–409	379.50–409.50	8	11
410–439	409.50–439.50	10	21
440–469	439.50–469.50	13	34
470–499	469.50–499.50	33	67
500–529	499.50–529.50	40	107
530–559	529.50–559.50	35	142
560–589	559.50–589.50	30	172
590–619	589.50–619.50	16	188
620–649	619.50–649.50	12	200
		Total 200	

Table 2-2 Cumulative frequency distribution of apartment rental rates

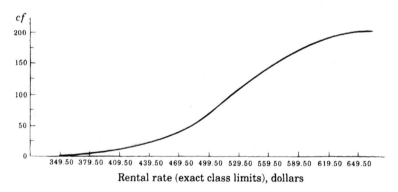

Rental rate (exact class limits), dollars

Figure 2-3

Solved Problem 2.5 Given that frequency curve (*a*) in Figure 2-4 is both symmetrical and mesokurtic, describe curves (*b*), (*c*), (*d*), (*e*), and (*f*) in terms of skewness and kurtosis.

Solution

Curve (*b*) is symmetrical and leptokurtic; curve (*c*), positively skewed and mesokurtic; curve (*d*), negatively skewed and mesokurtic; curve (*e*), symmetrical and platykurtic; and curve (*f*), positively skewed and leptokurtic.

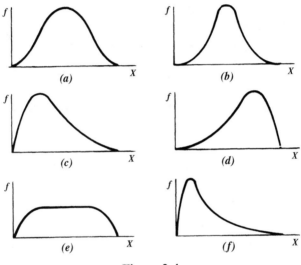

Figure 2-4

Chapter 3

DESCRIBING BUSINESS DATA: MEASURES OF LOCATION

In This Chapter:

- ✔ *Measures of Location in Data Sets*
- ✔ *The Arithmetic Mean*
- ✔ *The Weighted Mean*
- ✔ *The Median*
- ✔ *The Mode*
- ✔ *Relationship between the Mean and Median*
- ✔ *Mathematical Criteria Satisfied by the Median and the Mean*
- ✔ *Use of the Mean, Median, and Mode*
- ✔ *Use of the Mean in Statistical Process Control*

✔ *Quartiles, Deciles, and Percentiles*
✔ *Solved Problems*

Measures of Location in Data Sets

A measure of location is a value that is calculated for a group of data and that is used to describe the data in some way. Typically, we wish the value to be representative of all of the values in the group, and thus some kind of average is desired. In the statistical sense an *average* is a *measure of central tendency* for a collection of values. This chapter covers the various statistical procedures concerned with measures of location.

The Arithmetic Mean

The *arithmetic mean,* or *arithmetic average*, is defined as the sum of the values in the data group divided by the number of values.

In statistics, a descriptive measure of a population, or a *population parameter*, is typically represented by a Greek letter, whereas a descriptive measure of a sample, or a *sample statistic*, is represented by a Roman letter. Thus, the arithmetic mean for a population of values is represented by the symbol μ (read "mew"), while the arithmetic mean for a sample of values is represented by the symbol $\overline{X}$ (read "X bar"). The formulas for the sample mean and the population mean are:

$$\overline{X} = \sum X / n$$
$$\mu = \sum X / N$$

Operationally, the two formulas are identical; in both cases one sums all of the values ($\sum X$) and then divides by the number of values. However, the distinction in the denominators is that in statistical analysis the lowercase n indicates the number of items in the sample while the uppercase N typically indicates the number of items in the population.

The Weighted Mean

The *weighted mean* or *weighted average* is an arithmetic mean in which each value is weighted according to its importance in the overall group. The formulas for the population and sample weighted means are identical:

$$\mu_w \ op \ \bar{X}_w = \frac{\Sigma(wX)}{\Sigma w}$$

Operationally, each value in the group (X) is multiplied by the appropriate weight factor (w), and the products are then summed and divided by the sum of the weights.

⭐ Note!

The formulas for the sample mean and population mean are as follows:

$$\bar{X} = \Sigma X / n$$
$$\mu = \Sigma X / N$$

The Median

The *median* of a group items is the value of the middle item when all the items in the group are arranged in either ascending or descending order, in terms of value. For a group with an even number of items, the median is assumed to be midway between the two values adjacent to the middle. When a large number of values is contained in the group, the following formula to determine the position of the median in the ordered group is useful:

$$Med = X_{[(n/2) + (1/2)]}$$

The Mode

The *mode* is the value that occurs most frequently in a set of values. Such a distribution is described as being *unimodal*. For a small data set in which no measured values are repeated, there is no mode. When two non-adjoining values are about equal in having maximum frequencies associated with them, the distribution is described as being *bimodal*. Distributions of measurements with several modes are referred to as being *multimodal*.

Relationship between the Mean and Median

For any symmetrical distribution, the mean, median, and mode all coincide in value (see Figure 3-1 (a) below). For a positively skewed distribution the mean is always larger than the median (see Figure 3-1 (b) below). For a negatively skewed distribution the mean is always smaller

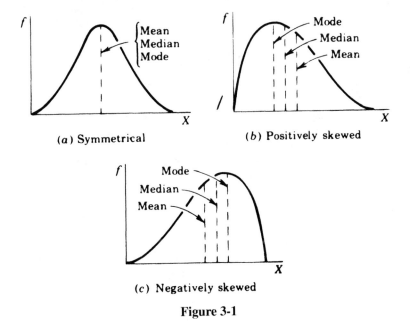

(a) Symmetrical

(b) Positively skewed

(c) Negatively skewed

Figure 3-1

than the median (see Figure 3-1 (c) below). These latter two relationships are always true, regardless of whether the distribution is unimodal or not.

Mathematical Criteria Satisfied by the Median and the Mean

One purpose for determining any measure of central tendency, such as a median or mean, is to use it to represent the general level of the values included in the group. Both the median and the mean are "good" representative measures, but from the standpoint of different mathematical criteria or objectives. The median is the representative value that minimizes the sum of the absolute values of the differences between each value in the group and the median. That is, the median minimizes the sum of the *absolute deviations* with respect to the individual values being represented. In contrast, the arithmetic mean focuses on minimizing the sum of the *squared deviations* with respect to the individual values in the group. The criterion by which the objective is that of minimizing the sum of the squared deviations associated with a representative value is called the *least-squares criterion*. This criterion is the one that is most important in statistical inference based on sample data.

Use of the Mean, Median, and Mode

We first consider the use of these measures of average for representing *population data*. The value of the mode indicates where most of the observed values are located. It can be useful as a descriptive measure for a population group, *but only if* there is one clear mode. On the other hand, the median is always an excellent measure by which to represent the "typical" level of observed values in a population. This is true regardless of whether there is more than one mode or whether the population distribution is skewed or symmetrical. The lack of symmetry is no special problem because the median wage rate, for example, is always the wage rate of the "middle person" when the wage rates are listed in order of magnitude. The arithmetic mean is also an excellent representative value for a population, *but only if* the population is fairly symmetrical. For nonsymmetrical data, the extreme values will serve to distort the value of the mean as a representative value. Thus, the median is generally the best measure of data location for describing population data.

We now consider the use of the three measures of location with respect to *sample data*. Recall from Chapter 1 that the purpose of statistical inference with sample data is to make probability statements about the population from which the sample was selected. The mode is not a good measure of location with respect to sample data because its value can vary greatly from sample to sample. The median is better than the mode because its value is more stable from sample to sample. However, the value of the mean is the most stable of the measures.

Example 3.1 The wage rates of all 650 hourly employees in a manufacturing firm have been compiled. The best representative measure of the typical wage rate is the median, because a population is involved and the median is relatively unaffected by any lack of symmetry in the wage rates. In fact, such data as wage rates and salary amounts are likely to be positively skewed, with relatively few wage or salary amounts being exceptionally high and in the right tail of the distribution.

Use of the Mean in Statistical Process Control

We observed that a run chart is a plot of data values in the time-sequence order in which they were observed and that the values plotted can be individual values or averages of sequential samples. We prefer to plot averages rather than individual values because any average generally will be more stable from sample to sample than will be the median or the mode. For this reason, the focus of run charts concerned with sample averages is to plot the sample means. Such a chart is called an $\bar{X}$ chart, and serves as the basis for determining whether a process is stable or whether there is process variation with an assignable cause that should be corrected.

Quartiles, Deciles, and Percentiles

Quartiles, deciles, and percentiles are similar to the median in that they also subdivide a distribution of measurements according to the proportion of frequencies observed. Whereas the median divides a distribution into halves, quartiles divides it into quarters, deciles divides it into tenths, and percentile points divide it into 100 parts. The formula for the median is modified according to the fraction point of interest. For example,

$$Q_1(\text{first quartile}) = X_{[(n/4) + (1/2)]}$$
$$D_3(\text{third decile}) = X_{[(3n/10) + (1/2)]}$$
$$P_{70}(\text{seventieth percentile}) = X_{[(70n/100) + (1/2)]}$$

Solved Problems

Solved Problem 3.1 For a sample of 15 students at an elementary school snack bar, the following sales amounts arranged in ascending order of magnitude are observed: $.10, .10, .25, .25, .25, .35, .40, .53, .90, 1.25, 1.35, 2.45, 2.71, 3.09, 4.10. Determine the (a) mean, (b) median, and (c) mode for these sales amounts.

Solution
(a) Mean = $1.21
(b) Median = $0.53
(c) Mode = most frequent value = $0.25

Solved Problem 3.2 How would you describe the distribution in Problem 3.1 from the standpoint of skewness?

Solution
With the mean being substantially larger than the median, the distribution of values is clearly positively skewed or skewed to the right.

Solved Problem 3.3 For the data in Solved Problem 3.1, suppose that you are asked to determine the typical purchase amount only for this particular group of students. Which measure of average would you report? Why?

Solution
Note that once we decide to focus only on this particular group, we are treating this group as our population of interest. Therefore, the best choice is to report the median as being the typical value; this is the eighth value in the array, or $0.53.

Solved Problem 3.4 Refer to Problem 3.3 above. Suppose we wish to estimate the typical amount of purchase in the population from which the sample was taken. Which measure of average would you report? Why?

Solution

Because statistical inference for a population is involved, our main concern is to report an average that is the most stable and has the least variability from sample to sample. The average that satisfied this requirement is the mean, because it satisfies the least-squares criterion. Therefore, the value reported should be the sample mean, or $1.21.

Solved Problem 3.5 A sample of 20 production workers in a company earned the following net pay amounts after all deductions for a given week: $240, 240, 240, 240, 240, 240, 240, 240, 255, 255, 265, 265, 280, 280, 290, 300, 305, 325, 330, 340. Calculate the (a) mean, (b) median, and (c) mode for this group of wages.

Solution
(a) Mean = $270.50
(b) Median = $260.00
(c) Mode = most frequent value = $240.00

Chapter 4
DESCRIBING BUSINESS DATA: MEASURES OF DISPERSION

✔ *Use of the Range and Standard Deviation in Statistical Process Control*
✔ *The Coefficient of Variation*
✔ *Pearson's Coefficient of Skewness*
✔ *Solved Problems*

Measures of Dispersion in Data Sets

The measures of central tendency described in Chapter 3 are useful for identifying the "typical" value in a group of values. In contrast, *measures of dispersion*, or *variability*, are concerned with describing the variability among the values. Several techniques are available for measuring the extent of variability in data sets. The ones described in this chapter are the *range, modified ranges, average deviation, variance, standard deviation*, and *coefficient of variation*.

The Range and Modified Ranges

The *range*, or *R*, is the difference between highest and lowest values included in a data set. Thus, when *H* represents the highest value in the group and *L* represents the lowest value, the range for ungrouped data is: $R = H - L$.

A *modified range* is a range for which some of the extreme values at each end of the distribution are eliminated from consideration. The middle 50 percent is the range between the values at the 25th percentile point and the 75th percentile point of the distribution. As such, it is also the range between the first and third quartiles of the distribution. For this reason, the middle 50 percent range is usually designated as the *interquartile range (IQR)*. Thus,

$$IQR = Q_3 - Q_1$$

Other modified ranges that are sometimes used are the middle 80 percent, middle 90 percent, and middle 95 percent.

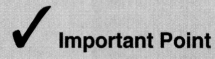

Important Point

A *box plot* is a graph that portrays the distribution of a data set by reference to the values at the quartiles as location measures and the value of the interquartile range as the reference measure of variability. A box plot is a relatively easy way of graphing data and observing the extent of skewness in the distribution.

The Mean Absolute Deviation

The *mean absolute deviation*, or *MAD*, is based on the absolute value of the difference between each value in the data set and the mean of the group. The mean average of these absolute values is then determined. It is sometimes called the "average deviation." The absolute values of the differences are used because the sum of all of the plus and minus differences (rather than the absolute differences) is always equal to zero. Thus the respective formulas for the population and sample MAD are:

Population $MAD = \dfrac{\Sigma |X - \mu|}{N}$

Sample $MAD = \dfrac{\Sigma |X - \bar{X}|}{n}$

The Variance and Standard Deviation

The *variance* is similar to the mean absolute deviation in that it is based on the difference between each value in the data set and the mean of the group. It differs in one very important way: each difference is *squared* before being summed. For a population, the variance is represented by $V(X)$ or, more typically, by the lowercase Greek σ^2 (read "sigma squared"). The formula is:

$$V(X) = \sigma^2 = \frac{\Sigma(X - \mu)^2}{N}$$

Unlike the situation for other sample statistics we have discussed, the variance for a sample is not computationally exactly equivalent to the variance for a population. Rather, the denominator in the sample variance formula is slightly different. Essentially, a correction factor is included in this formula, so that the sample variance is an unbiased estimator of the population variance. The sample variance is represented by s^2; its formula is:

$$s^2 = \frac{\Sigma(X - \overline{X})^2}{n-1}$$

In general, it is difficult to interpret the meaning of the value of a variance because the units in which it is expressed are squared values. Partly for this reason, the square root of the variance, represented by the Greek σ (or s for a sample) and called the *standard deviation* is more frequently used. The formulas are:

Population standard deviation: $\sigma = \sqrt{\dfrac{\Sigma(X - \mu)^2}{N}}$

Sample standard deviation: $s = \sqrt{\dfrac{\Sigma(X - \overline{X})^2}{n-1}}$

 **Note!**

The standard deviation is particularly useful in conjunction with the so-called normal distribution.

Simplified Calculations for the Variance and Standard Deviation

The formulas in the preceding section are called *deviations formulas*, because in each case the specific deviations of individual values from the mean must be determined. Alternative formulas, which are mathematically equivalent but which do not require the determination of each deviation, have been derived. Because these formulas are generally easier to use for computations, they are called *computational formulas*. The computational formulas are:

Population variance: $\sigma^2 = \dfrac{\Sigma X^2 - N\mu^2}{N}$

Population standard deviation: $\sigma = \sqrt{\dfrac{\Sigma X^2 - N\mu^2}{N}}$

Sample Variance: $s^2 = \dfrac{\Sigma X^2 - n\overline{X}^2}{n-1}$

Sample standard deviation: $s = \sqrt{\dfrac{\Sigma X^2 - n\overline{X}^2}{n-1}}$

Mathematical Criterion Associated with the Variance and Standard Deviation

In Chapter 3 we described the least-squares criterion and established that the arithmetic mean is the measure of data location that satisfies this criterion. Now refer to the formula for population variance and note that the variance is in fact a type of arithmetic mean, in that it is the sum of squared deviations divided by the number of such values. From this standpoint alone, the variance is thereby associated with the least-squares criterion. Note also that the sum of the squared deviations in the numerator of the variance formula is precisely the sum that is minimized when the arithmetic mean is used as the measure of location. Therefore, the variance and its square root, the standard deviation, have a close mathematical relationship with the mean, and both are used in statistical inference with sample data.

Use of the Standard Deviation in Data Description

As established in the preceding section, the standard deviation is used in conjunction with a number of methods of statistical inference covered in later chapters of this book. A description of these methods is beyond the scope of the present chapter. However, aside from the uses of the standard deviation in inference, we can now briefly introduce a use of the standard deviation in data description.

Consider a distribution of data values that is both symmetrical and mesokurtic. The frequency curve for such a distribution is called a normal curve. For a set of values that is normally distributed, it is always true that approximately 68 percent of the values are included within one standard deviation of the mean and approximately 95 percent of the values are included within two standard deviation units of the mean. These observations are presented diagrammatically in Figures 4-1(a) and (b), respectively. Thus, in addition to the mean and standard deviation both being associated with the least-squares criterion, they are also mutually used in analyses for normally distributed variables.

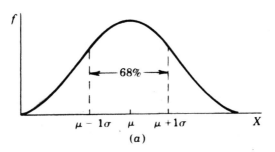

Figure 4-1(a)

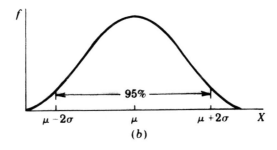

Figure 4-1(b)

Use of the Range and Standard Deviation in Statistical Process Control

As introduced in Chapter 3, the sample mean is used in process control for averages by the construction of $\overline{X}$ charts. In addition to controlling process averages, there is at least an equal interest in controlling process variability. To monitor and control variability, either the ranges or the standard deviations of the rational subgroups that constitute the sequential samples are determined. In either case, the values are plotted identically in form to the run chart for the sequence of sample mean weights. Such a chart for sample ranges is called an *R chart*, while the chart for sample standard deviations is called an *s chart*.

From the standpoint of using the measure of variability that is most stable, the least-squares oriented *s chart* is preferred. Historically, the range has been used most frequently for monitoring process variability because it can be easily determined with little calculation. However, availability of more sophisticated weighing devices that are programmed to calculate both the sample mean and standard deviation has resulted in greater use of *s* charts.

The Coefficient of Variation

The *coefficient of variation*, CV, indicates the relative magnitude of the standard deviation as compared with the mean of the distribution of measurements, as a percentage. Thus, the formulas are:

Population: $CV = \dfrac{\sigma}{\mu} \times 100$

Sample: $CV = \dfrac{s}{\overline{X}} \times 100$

> # Remember
>
> The coefficient of variation is useful when we wish to compare the variability of two data sets relative to the general level of values (and thus relative to the mean) in each set.

Pearson's Coefficient of Skewness

Pearson's *coefficient of skewness* measures the departure from symmetry by expressing the difference between the mean and the median relative to the standard deviation of the group of measurements. The formulas are:

$$\text{Population skewness} = \frac{3(\mu - Med)}{\sigma}$$

$$\text{Sample skewness} = \frac{3(\overline{X} - Med)}{s}$$

For a symmetrical distribution the value of the coefficient of skewness will always be zero, because the mean and median are equal to one another in value. For a positively skewed distribution, the mean is always larger than the median; hence, the value of the coefficient is positive. For a negatively skewed distribution, the mean is always smaller than the median; hence, the value of the coefficient is negative.

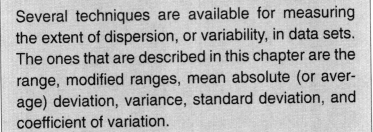

You Need to Know ✔

Several techniques are available for measuring the extent of dispersion, or variability, in data sets. The ones that are described in this chapter are the range, modified ranges, mean absolute (or average) deviation, variance, standard deviation, and coefficient of variation.

Solved Problems

Solved Problem 4.1 For a sample of 15 students at an elementary school snack bar, the following sales amounts, arranged in ascending order of magnitude, are observed: $0.10, 0.10, 0.25, 0.25, 0.25, 0.35, 0.40, 0.53, 0.90, 1.25, 1.35, 2.45, 2.71, 3.09, 4.10. Determine the (a) range and (b) interquartile range for these sample data.

Solution: (a) $4.00 (b) $1.925

Solved Problem 4.2 Compute the mean absolute deviation for the data in Solved Problem 4.1. The sample mean for this group of values was determined to be $1.21 in Solved Problem 3.1.

Solution: Using Table 4.1, the average deviation is $1.03.

X	$X - \bar{X}$	$\lvert X - \bar{X} \rvert$
$0.10	$ -1.11	$1.11
0.10	-1.11	1.11
0.25	-0.96	0.96
0.25	-0.96	0.96
0.25	-0.96	0.96
0.35	-0.86	0.86
0.40	-0.81	0.81
0.53	-0.68	0.68
0.90	-0.31	0.31
1.25	0.04	0.04
1.35	0.14	0.14
2.45	1.24	1.24
2.71	1.50	1.50
3.09	1.88	1.88
4.10	2.89	2.89
	Total	$15.45

Table 4.1 Worksheet for calculating the mean absolute deviation for the snack bar data

Solved Problem 4.3 Determine the sample standard deviation for the data in Solved Problems 4.1 and 4.2 by using (a) the deviations formula and (b) the alternative computational formula, and demonstrate that the answers are equivalent.

Solution: (a) $s = \$1.28$ (b) $s = \$1.27$

X	$X - \bar{X}$	$(X - \bar{X})^2$	X^2
\$0.10	\$-1.11	1.2321	0.0100
0.10	-1.11	1.2321	0.0100
0.25	-0.96	0.9216	0.0625
0.25	-0.96	0.9216	0.0625
0.25	-0.96	0.9216	0.0625
0.35	-0.86	0.7396	0.1225
0.40	-0.81	0.6561	0.1600
0.53	-0.68	0.4624	0.2809
0.90	-0.31	0.0961	0.8100
1.25	0.04	0.0016	1.5625
1.35	0.14	0.0196	1.8225
2.45	1.24	1.5376	6.0025
2.71	1.50	2.2500	7.3441
3.09	1.88	3.5344	9.5481
4.10	2.89	8.3521	16.8100
		Total 22.8785	Total 44.6706

Table 4.2 Worksheet for calculating the sample standard deviation for the snack bar data

Solved Problem 4.4 Many national academic achievement and aptitude tests, such as the SAT, report standardized test scores with the mean for the normative group used to establish scoring standards converted to 500 with a standard deviation of 100. Suppose that the distribution of scores for such a test is known to be approximately normally distributed. Determine the approximate percentage of reported scores that would be between (a) 400 and 600 and (b) between 500 and 700.

Solution: (a) 68% (b) 47.5% (i.e., one-half of the middle 95%)

Solved Problem 4.5 Referring to the standardized achievement test in Solved Problem 4.4, what are the percentile values that would be reported for scores of (a) 400, (b) 500, (c) 600 and (d) 700?

Solution: (a) 16, (b) 50, (c) 84, and (d) 97.5

Chapter 5
PROBABILITY

Basic Definitions of Probability

Historically, three different conceptual approaches have been developed for defining probability and for determining probability values: the classical, relative frequency, and subjective approaches. By the *classical approach* to probability, if $N(A)$ possible elementary outcomes are favorable to event A, $N(S)$ possible outcomes are included in the sample space, and all the elementary outcomes are equally likely and mutually exclusive, then the probability that event A will occur is:

$$P(A) = N(A)/N(S)$$

Note that the classical approach to probability is based on the assumption that each outcome is equally likely. Because this approach (when it is applicable) permits determination of probability values before any sample events are observed, it has been called the *a priori approach*.

By the *relative frequency approach*, the probability is determined on the basis of the proportion of times that a favorable outcome occurs in a number of observations or experiments. No prior assumption of equal likelihood is involved. Because determination of the probability values is based on observation and collection of data, this approach has also been called the *empirical approach*. The probability that event A will occur by the relative frequency approach is:

$$P(A) = n(A)/n$$

Both the classical and relative frequency approaches yield *objective* probability values, in the sense that the probability values indicate the relative rate of occurrence of the event in the long run. In contrast, the *subjective approach* to probability is particularly appropriate when there is only one opportunity for the event to occur, and it will either occur or not occur that one time. By the subjective approach, the probability of an event is the *degree of belief* by an individual that the event will occur, based on all evidence available to the individual. Because the probability value is a personal judgment, the subjective approach has also been called the *personalistic approach*. This approach to probability has been developed relatively recently and is related to *decision analysis*.

Expressing Probability

The symbol *P* is used to designate the probability of an event. Thus $P(A)$ denotes the probability that event *A* will occur in a single observation or experiment. The smallest value that a probability statement can have is 0 (indicating the event is impossible) and the largest value it can have is 1 (indicating the event is certain to occur). Thus, in general, $0 \leq P(A) \leq 1$. In a given observation or experiment, an event must either occur or not occur. Therefore, the sum of the probability of occurrence plus the probability of nonoccurrence always equals 1. Thus, where A' indicates the nonoccurrence of event *A*, we have $P(A) + P(A') = 1$.

A *Venn diagram* is a diagram related to set theory in mathematics by which the events that can occur in a particular observation or experiment can be portrayed. An enclosed figure represents a sample space, and portions of the area within the space are designated to represent particular elementary or composite events, or event spaces.

As an alternative to probability values, probabilities can also be expressed in terms of *odds*. The odds ratio favoring the occurrence of an event is the ratio of the relative number of outcomes, designated by *a*, that are favorable to *A*, to the relative number of outcomes, designated by *b*, that are not favorable to *A*:

$$\text{Odds} = a{:}b \text{ (read ``}a\text{ to }b\text{'')}$$

Mutually Exclusive and Nonexclusive Events

Two or more events are *mutually exclusive*, or *disjoint*, if they cannot occur together. That is, the occurrence of one event automatically precludes the occurrence of the other event.

Two or more events are *nonexclusive* when it is possible for them to occur together.

Note!

This definition does not indicate that such events must necessarily always occur jointly.

For instance, suppose we consider the two possible events "ace" and "king" with respect to a card being drawn from a deck of playing cards. These two events are mutually exclusive, because any given card cannot be both an ace and a king. Suppose we consider the two possible events "ace" and "spade." These events are not mutually exclusive, because a given card can be both an ace and a spade; however, it does not follow that every ace is a spade or every spade is an ace.

The Rules of Addition

The rules of addition are used when we wish to determine the probability of one event or another (or both) occurring in a single observation. Symbolically, we can represent the probability of event A or event B occurring by $P(A$ or $B)$. In the language of set theory this is called the *union* of A and B and the probability is designated by $P(A \cup B)$ (read "probability of A union B"). There are two variations of the rule of addition, depending on whether or not the two events are mutually exclusive. The rule of addition for mutually exclusive events is $P(A$ or $B) = P(A \cup B) = P(A) + P(B)$.

For events that are *not* mutually exclusive, the probability of the joint occurrence of the two events is subtracted from the sum of the simple probabilities of the two events. We can represent the probability of joint occurrence by $P(A$ and $B)$. In the language of set theory this is called the *intersection* of A and B and the probability is designated by $P(A \cap B)$ (read "probability of A intersect B"). Thus, the rule of addition for events that are not mutually exclusive is $P(A$ or $B) = P(A) + P(B) - P(A$ and $B)$. That formula is also often called the *general rule of addition*, because for events that are mutually exclusive the last term would always be zero, resulting in the formula then being equivalent to the formula for mutually exclusive events.

Venn diagrams can be used to portray the rationale underlying the two rules of addition. In Figure 5-1(a), note that the probability of *A* or *B* occurring is conceptually equivalent to adding the proportion of area included in *A* and *B*. In Figure 5-1(b), for events that are not mutually exclusive, some elementary events are included in both *A* and *B*; thus there is overlap between these event sets. When the areas included in *A* and *B* are added together for events that are not mutually exclusive, the area of overlap is essentially added in twice. Thus, the rationale of subtracting *P*(*A* and *B*) in the rule of addition for nonexclusive events is to correct the sum for the duplicate addition of the intersect area.

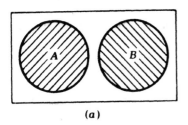 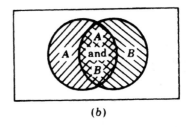

(a)   **(b)**

Figure 5-1

Independent Events, Dependent Events, and Conditional Probability

Two events are *independent* when the occurrence or nonoccurrence of one event has no effect on the probability of occurrence of the other event. Two events are *dependent* when the occurrence or nonoccurrence of one event does affect the probability of occurrence of the other event.

When two events are dependent, the concept of *conditional probability* is employed to designate the probability of occurrence of the related event. The expression *P*(*B*|*A*) indicates the probability of event *B* occurring given that event *A* has occurred. Note that *B*|*A* is not a fraction.

Conditional probability expressions are not required for independent events because by definition there is no relationship between the occurrence of such events. Therefore, if events *A* and *B* are independent, the conditional probability *P*(*B*|*A*) is always equal to simple probability *P*(*B*). If the simple probability of a first event *A* and the joint probability of two events A and B are known, then the conditional probability $P(B|A)$ can be determined by:

$$P(B|A) = P(A \text{ and } B)/P(A)$$

There is often some confusion regarding the distinction between mutually exclusive and nonexclusive events on the one hand, and the concepts of independence and dependence on the other hand. Particularly, note the difference between events that are mutually exclusive and events that are independent. Mutual exclusiveness indicates that two events cannot both occur, whereas independence indicates that the probability of occurrence of one event is not affected by the occurrence of the other event. Therefore it follows that if two events are mutually exclusive, this is a particular example of highly dependent events, because the probability of one event given that the other has occurred would always be equal to zero.

The Rules of Multiplication

The rules of multiplication are concerned with determining the probability of the joint occurrence of A and B. This concerns the intersection of A and B: $P(A \cap B)$. There are two variations of the rule of multiplication, according to whether the two events are independent or dependent. The rule of multiplication for independent events is:

$$P(A \text{ and } B) = P(A \cap B) = P(A)P(B)$$

For dependent events the probability of the joint occurrence of A and B is the probability of A multiplied by the *conditional* probability of B given A. An equivalent value is obtained if the two events are reversed in position. Thus the rule of multiplication for dependent events is:

$$P(A \text{ and } B) = P(A)P(B|A); \text{ or } P(A \text{ and } B) = P(B \text{ and } A) = P(B)P(A|B)$$

The first formula is often called the *general rule of multiplication*, because for events that are independent the conditional probability $P(B|A)$ is always equal to the unconditional probability value $P(B)$, resulting in the formula being equivalent to the formula for independent events.

Bayes' Theorem

In its simplest algebraic form, Bayes' theorem is concerned with determining the conditional probability of event A given that event B has occurred. The general form of Bayes' theorem is:

$$P(A|B) = P(A \text{ and } B)/P(B)$$

This formula is simply a particular application of the general formula for conditional probability. However, the special importance of Bayes' theorem is that it is applied in the context of sequential events, and further, that the computational version of the formula provides the basis for determining the conditional probability of an event having occurred in the first sequential position given that a particular event has been observed in the second sequential position.

Joint Probability Tables

A *joint probability table* is a table in which all possible events for one variable are listed as row headings, all possible events for a second variable are listed as column headings, and the value entered in each cell of the table is the probability of each joint occurrence. Often, the probabilities in such a table are based on observed frequencies of occurrence for the various joint events, rather than being *a priori* in nature. The table of joint-occurrence frequencies that can serve as the basis for constructing a joint probability table is called a *contingency table*. In the context of joint probability tables, a *marginal probability* is so named because it is a marginal total of a row or a column. Whereas the probability values in the cells are probabilities of joint occurrence, the marginal probabilities are the unconditional, or simple, probabilities of particular events.

Permutations

By the classical approach to determining probabilities presented earlier in the chapter, the probability value is based on the ratio of the number of equally likely elementary outcomes that are favorable to the total number of outcomes in the sample space. When the problems are simple, the number of elementary outcomes can be counted directly. However, for more complex problems the methods of permutations and combinations are required to determine the number of possible elementary outcomes.

The number of *permutations* of n objects is the number of ways in which the objects can be arranged in terms of order:

Permutations of n objects $= n! = (n) \times (n-1) \times \cdots \times (2) \times (1)$

The symbol $n!$ is read "n factorial." In permutations and combinations problems, n is always positive. Also, note that by definition $0! = 1$ in mathematics.

Typically, we are concerned about the number of permutations of some subgroup of the n objects, rather than all n objects as such. That is, we are interested in the number of permutations of n objects taken r at a time, where r is less than n:

$$_nP_r = n!/(n-r)!$$

Combinations

In the case of permutations, the order in which the objects are arranged is important. In the case of *combinations*, we are concerned with the number of different groupings of objects that can occur *without* regard to their order. Therefore, an interest in combinations always concerns the number of different subgroups that can be taken from n objects. The number of combinations of n objects taken r at a time is:

$$_nC_r = n!/r!(n-r)!$$

As indicated earlier in the chapter, the methods of permutations and combinations provide a basis for counting the possible outcomes in relatively complex situations. In terms of combinations, we can frequently determine the probability of an event by determining the number of combinations of outcomes that include that event as compared with the total number of combinations that are possible. Of course, this again represents the classical approach to probability and is based on the assumption that all combinations are equally likely.

Solved Problems

Solved Problem 5.1 For each of the following situations, indicate whether the classical, relative frequency, or subjective approach would be most useful for determining the required probability value.

(a) Probability that there will be a recession next year.

(b) Probability that a six-sided die will show either a 6 or 1.

(c) Probability that a randomly chosen person who enters a large department store will make a purchase in that store.

Solution: (a) subjective, (b) classical, and (c) relative frequency

Solved Problem 5.2 Determine the probability of obtaining an ace (A), king (K), or a deuce (D) when one card is drawn from a well-shuffled deck of 52 playing cards.

Solution: $P(A$ or K or $D) = P(A) + P(K) + P(D) = 3/13$

Solved Problem 5.3 In general, the probability that a prospect will make a purchase after being contacted by a salesperson is $P = 0.40$. If a salesperson selects three prospects randomly from a file and makes contact with them, what is the probability that all three prospects will make a purchase?

Solution: P(all are purchasers) $= (0.40) \times (0.40) \times (0.40) = 0.064$

Chapter 6
PROBABILITY DISTRIBUTIONS FOR DISCRETE RANDOM VARIABLES: BINOMIAL, HYPERGEOMETRIC, AND POISSON

IN THIS CHAPTER:

- ✔ What Is a Random Variable?
- ✔ Describing a Discrete Random Variable
- ✔ The Binomial Distribution
- ✔ The Binomial Variable Expressed by Proportions
- ✔ The Hypergeometric Distribution

✔ *The Poisson Distribution*
✔ *Poisson Approximation of Binomial Probabilities*
✔ *Solved Problems*

What Is a Random Variable?

In contrast to categorical events, such as drawing
a particular card from a deck of cards, a *random
variable* is a *numerical* event whose value is determined by a chance process. When probability
values are assigned to all possible numerical values of a random variable X, either by a listing or
by a mathematical function, the result is a *prob-
ability distribution*. The sum of the probabilities for all the possible numerical outcomes must equal 1.0. Individual probability values may be
denoted by the symbol $f(x)$, which indicates that a mathematical function
is involved, by $P(x = X)$, which recognizes that the random variable can
have various specific values, or simply by $P(X)$.

For a *discrete random variable*, observed values can occur only at
isolated points along a scale of values. Therefore, it is possible that all numerical values for the variable can be listed in a table with accompanying probabilities. There are several standard probability distributions that
can serve as models for a wide variety of discrete random variables involved in business applications. The standard models described in this
chapter are the binomial, hypergeometric, and Poisson probability distributions.

For a *continuous random variable*, all possible fractional values of
the variable cannot be listed, and therefore, the probabilities that are determined by a mathematical function are portrayed graphically by a probability density function or probability curve.

Describing a Discrete Random Variable

Just as for collections of sample and population data, it is often useful to
describe a random variable in terms of its *mean* and its *variance*, or *stan-*

dard deviation. The (long-run) mean for a random variable X is called the *expected value* and is denoted by $E(X)$. For a discrete random variable, it is the weighted average of all possible numerical values of the variable with the respective probabilities used as weights. Because the sum of the weights (probabilities) is 1.0, the following formula can be simplified, and the expected value for a discrete random variable is:

$$E(X) = \sum XP(X)$$

The variance of a random variable X is denoted by $V(X)$; it is computed with respect to $E(X)$ as the mean of the probability distribution. The general deviations form of the formula for the variance of a discrete random variable is:

$$V(X) = \sum [X - E(X)]^2 P(X)$$

The computational form of the formula for the variance of a discrete random variable, which does not require the determination of deviations from the mean, is:

$$V(X) = \sum X^2 P(X) - [\sum XP(X)]^2$$
$$= E(X^2) - [E(X)]^2$$

The standard deviation for a random variable is simply the square root of the variance:

$$\sigma = \sqrt{V(X)}$$

 **Note!**

An advantage of the standard deviation is that it is expressed in the same units as the random variable, rather than being in squared units.

The Binomial Distribution

The binomial distribution is a discrete probability distribution that is applicable as a model for decision-making situations in which a sampling process can be assumed to conform to a Bernoulli process. A *Bernoulli process* is a sampling process in which:

1. Only two mutually exclusive possible outcomes are possible in each trial, or observation. For convenience these are called *success* and *failure.*
2. The outcomes in the series of trials, or observations, constitute *independent events.*
3. The probability of success in each trial, denoted by p, remains constant from trial to trial. That is, the process is stationary.

The binomial distribution can be used to determine the probability of obtaining a designated number of successes in a Bernoulli process. Three values are required: the designated number of successes (X); the number of trials, or observations (n); and the probability of success in each trial (p). Where $q = (1 - p)$, the formula for determining the probability of a specific number of successes X for a binomial distribution is:

$$P(X\, n, p) = {}_nC_X\, p^X q^{n-X}$$
$$= \frac{n!}{X!(n-X)!}\, p^X q^{n-X}$$

Often there is an interest in the cumulative probability of "X or more" successes or "X or fewer" successes occurring in n trials. In such a case, the probability of each outcome included within the designated interval must be determined, and then these probabilities are summed.

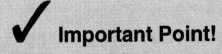 **Important Point!**

Because use of the binomial formula involves considerable arithmetic when the sample is relatively large, tables of binomial probabilities are often used.

The values of p referenced in a table of binomial probabilities typically do not exceed $p = 0.50$. If the value of p in a particular application exceeds 0.50, the problem is restated so that the event is defined in terms of the number of failures rather than the number of successes.

The expected value (long-run mean) and variance for a given binomial distribution could be determined by listing the probability distribution in a table and applying the formulas presented earlier in the chapter. However, the expected number of successes can be computed directly:

$$E(X) = np$$

Where $q = (1 - p)$, the variance of the number of successes can also be computed directly:

$$V(X) = npq$$

The Binomial Variable Expressed by Proportions

Instead of expressing the random binomial variable as the number of successes X, we can designate it in terms of the proportion of successes $\hat{p}$, which is the ratio of the number of successes to the number of trials:

$$\hat{p} = X/n$$

In such cases, the formula is modified only with respect to defining the proportion. Thus, the probability of observing exactly $\hat{p}$ proportion of successes in n Bernouilli trials is:

$$P(\hat{p} = X/n \mid n,p) = {}_nC_X p^X q^{n-X}$$
$$P(\hat{p} = X/n \mid n,\pi) = {}_nC_X \pi^X (1 - \pi)^{n-X}$$

In the second formula, π is the equivalent of p except that it specifically indicates that the probability of success in an individual trial is a population or process parameter.

When the binomial variable is expressed as a proportion, the distribution is still discrete and not continuous. Only the particular proportions for which the number of successes X is a whole number can occur. The expected value for a binomial probability distribution expressed by proportions is equal to the population proportion, which may be designated by either p or π:

$$E(\hat{p}) = p \quad \text{or} \quad E(\hat{p}) = \pi$$

The variance of the proportion of successes for a binomial probability distribution, when $q = (1 - p)$, is:

$$V(\hat{p}) = pq/n \quad \text{or} \quad V(\hat{p}) = \pi(1 - \pi)/n$$

The Hypergeometric Distribution

When sampling is done *without replacement* of each sampled item taken from a finite population of items, the Bernoulli process does not apply because there is a systematic change in the probability of success as items are removed from the population.

Don't Forget!

When sampling without replacement is used in a situation that would otherwise qualify as a Bernoulli process, the hypergeometric distribution is the appropriate discrete probability distribution.

The Poisson Distribution

The *Poisson distribution* can be used to determine the probability of a designated number of events occurring when the events occur in a continuum of time or space. Such a process is called a *Poisson process*; it is similar to the Bernoulli process except that the events occur over a continuum and there are no trials as such. An example of such a process is the arrival of incoming calls at a telephone switchboard. As was the case for the Bernoulli process, it is assumed that the events are independent and that the process is stationary.

Only one value is required to determine the probability of a designated number of events occurring in a Poisson process: the long-run mean number of events for the specific time or space dimension of interest. This mean generally is represented by λ (Greek lambda), or possibly by μ. The formula for determining the probability of a designated number of successes X in a Poisson distribution is:

$$P(X|\lambda)\frac{\lambda^X e^{-\lambda}}{X!}$$

Because a Poisson process is assumed to be stationary, it follows that the mean of the process is always proportional to the length of the time or space continuum. Therefore, if the mean is available for one length of time, the mean for any other required time period can be determined.

You Need to Know

This is important, because the value of λ that is used must apply to the time period of interest.

By definition, the expected value for a Poisson probability distribution is equal to the mean of the distribution: $E(X) = \lambda$.

As it happens, the variance of the number of events for a Poisson probability distribution is also equal to the mean of the distribution λ:

$$V(X) = \lambda$$

Poisson Approximation of Binomial Probabilities

When the number of observations or trials n in a Bernoulli process is large, computations are quite tedious. Further, tabled probabilities for very small values of p are not generally available. Fortunately, the Poisson distribution is suitable as an approximation of binomial probabilities when n is large and p or q is small. A convenient rule is that such approximation can be made when $n \geq 30$, and either $np < 5$ or $nq < 5$. Different texts use somewhat different rules for determining when such approximation is appropriate. The mean for the Poisson probability distribution that is used to approximate binomial probabilities is: $\lambda = np$.

When n is large but neither np nor nq is less than 5, binomial probabilities can be approximated by use of the normal probability distribution.

Solved Problems

Solved Problem 6.1 The number of trucks arriving hourly at a warehouse facility has been found to follow the probability in Table 6.1. Calculate (a) the expected number of arrivals X per hour, (b) the variance, and (c) the standard deviation for the discrete random variable.

Number of trucks (X)	0	1	2	3	4	5	6
Probability [$P(X)$]	0.05	0.10	0.15	0.25	0.30	0.10	0.05

Table 6.1 Hourly arrival of trucks at a warehouse

Solution: (a) $E(X) = 3.15$ trucks, (b) $V(X) = 2.1275$, and (c) $\sigma = 1.46$ trucks

Solved Problem 6.2 If a fair coin is tossed five times, the probability distribution with respect to the number of heads observed is based on the binomial distribution, with $n = 5$ and $p = 0.50$. Determine (a) the expected number of heads in five tosses and (b) the standard deviation of the number of heads by use of the special formulas applicable for binomial probability distributions.

Solution: (a) $E(X) = 2.50$ heads, (b) $\sigma = \sqrt{V(X)} = 1.12$ heads

Chapter 7

PROBABILITY DISTRIBUTIONS FOR CONTINUOUS RANDOM VARIABLES: NORMAL AND EXPONENTIAL

IN THIS CHAPTER:

- ✔ Continuous Random Variables
- ✔ The Normal Probability Distribution
- ✔ Normal Approximation of Binomial Probabilities
- ✔ Normal Approximation of Poisson Probabilities

✔ *The Exponential Probability Distribution*
✔ *Solved Problems*

Continuous Random Variables

As contrasted to a discrete random variable, a *continuous random variable* is one that can assume any fractional value within a defined range of values. Because there is an infinite number of possible fractional measurements, one cannot list every possible value with corresponding probability. Instead, a *probability density function* is defined. This mathematical expression gives the function of X, represented by the symbol $f(X)$, for any designated value of the random variable X. The plot for such a function is called a *probability curve*, and the area  between any two points under the curve indicates the probability of a value between these two points occurring by chance.

Several standard continuous probability distributions are applicable as models to a wide variety of continuous variables under designated circumstances. Probability tables have been prepared for these standard deviations, making it unnecessary to use the method of integration in order to determine areas under the probability curve for these distributions. The standard continuous probability models described in this chapter are the normal and exponential probability distributions.

The Normal Probability Distribution

The *normal probability distribution* is a continuous probability distribution that is *both symmetrical* and *mesokurtic*. The probability curve representing the normal probability distribution is often described as being bell-shaped. The normal probability distribution is important in statistical inference for three distinct reasons:

1. The measurements obtained in many random processes are known to follow this distribution.
2. Normal probabilities can often be used to approximate other probability distributions, such as the binomial and Poisson distributions.
3. Distributions of such statistics as the sample mean and sample proportion are normally distributed when the sample size is large, regardless of the distribution of the parent population.

As is true for any continuous probability distribution, a probability value for a continuous random variable can be determined only for an *interval* of values. The height of the density function, or probability curve, for a normally distributed variable is given by

$$f(X) = \frac{1}{\sqrt{2\pi\sigma^2}} e^{-[(X-\mu)^2/2\sigma^2]}$$

where π is the constant 3.1416, e is the constant 2.7183, μ is the mean of the distribution, and σ is the standard deviation of the distribution. Since every different combination of μ and σ would generate a different normal probability distribution (all symmetrical and mesokurtic), tables of normal probabilities are based on one particular distribution: *the standard normal distribution.* This is the normal probability distribution with $\mu = 0$ and $\sigma = 1$. Any value X from a normally distributed population can be converted into equivalent standard normal value z by the formula:

$$z = (X - \mu)/\sigma$$

Important!

Any z value restates the original value X in terms of the number of units of the standard deviation by which the original value differs from the mean of the distribution. A negative value of z would indicate that the original value X was below the value of the mean.

Normal Approximation of Binomial Probabilities

When the number of observations or trials n is relatively large, the normal probability distribution can be used to approximate binomial probabilities. A convenient rule is that such approximation is acceptable when $n \geq 30$, and both $np \geq 5$ and $nq \geq 5$. This rule, combined with the one for the Poisson approximation of binomial probabilities, means that whenever $n \geq 30$, binomial probabilities can be approximated by either the normal or the Poisson distribution, depending on the values of np and nq. Different texts use somewhat different rules for determining when such approximations are appropriate.

When the normal probability distribution is used as the basis for approximating a binomial probability value, the mean and standard deviation are based on the expected value and variance of the number of successes for the binomial distribution. The mean number of successes is: $\mu = np$.

The standard deviation of the number of successes is: $\sigma = \sqrt{npq}$.

Normal Approximation of Poisson Probabilities

When the mean λ of a Poisson distribution is relatively large, the normal probability distribution can be used to approximate Poisson probabilities. A convenient rule is that such approximation is acceptable when $\lambda \geq 10.0$.

The mean and standard deviation of the normal probability distribution are based on the expected value and the variance of the number of events in a Poisson process. This mean is: $\mu = \lambda$.

The standard deviation is: $\sigma = \sqrt{\lambda}$.

The Exponential Probability Distribution

If events occur in the context of a Poisson process, then the length of time or space between successive events follow an *exponential probability distribution*. Because the time or space is a continuum, such a measurement is a continuous random variable. As is the case of any continuous random variable, it is not meaningful to ask: "What is the probability that the first request for service will arrive in exactly one minute?" Rather, we must designate an *interval* within which the event is to occur, such as by asking: "What is the probability that the first request for service will arrive within a minute?"

Since the Poisson process is stationary, with equal likelihood of the event occurring throughout the relevant period of time, the exponential distribution applies whether we are concerned with the time (or space) until the very first event, the time between two successive events, or the time until the first event occurs after any selected point in time.

Where λ is the mean number of occurrences for the *interval of interest*, the exponential probability that the first event will occur within the designated interval of time and space is:

$$P(T \le t) = 1 - e^{-\lambda}$$

Similarly, the exponential probability that the first event *will not* occur within the designated interval of time or space is:

$$P(T > t) = e^{-\lambda}$$

Solved Problems

Solved Problem 7.1 The packaging process in a breakfast cereal company has been adjusted so that an average of $\mu = 13.0$ oz of cereal is placed in each package. Of course, not all packages have precisely 13.0 oz because of random sources of variability. The standard deviation of the actual net weight is $\sigma = 0.1$ oz, and the distribution of weights is known to follow the normal probability distribution. Determine the probability that a randomly chosen package will contain between 13.0 and 13.2 oz of cereal and illustrate the proportion of area under the normal curve that is associated with this probability value.

Solution:

$$z = \frac{X - \mu}{\sigma} = \frac{13.2 - 13.0}{0.1} = +2.0$$
$$P(13.0 \le X \le 13.2) = P(0 \le z \le +2.0) = 0.4772$$

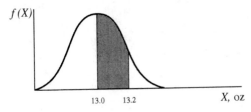

Figure 7-1

Solved Problem 7.2 For the situation described in Solved Problem 7.1, what is the probability that the weight of the cereal will exceed 13.25 oz? Illustrate the proportion of area under the normal curve that is relevant in this case.

Solution:

$$z = \frac{X - \mu}{\sigma} = \frac{13.25 - 13.0}{0.1} = +2.5$$

$$P(X > 13.25) = P(z > +2.5) = 0.5000 - 0.4938 = 0.0062$$

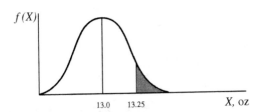

Figure 7-2

Chapter 8

SAMPLING DISTRIBUTIONS AND CONFIDENCE INTERVALS FOR THE MEAN

IN THIS CHAPTER:

- ✔ Point Estimation of a Population or Process Parameter
- ✔ The Concept of a Sampling Distribution
- ✔ Sampling Distribution of the Mean
- ✔ The Central Limit Theorem
- ✔ Determining Probability Values for the Sample Mean
- ✔ Confidence Intervals for the Mean Using the Normal Distribution

✔ *Determining the Required Sample Size for Estimating the Mean*
✔ *The* t *Distribution and Confidence Intervals for the Mean*
✔ *Summary Table for Interval Estimation of the Population Mean*
✔ *Solved Problems*

Point Estimation of a Population or Process Parameter

Because of factors such as time and cost, the parameters of a population or process frequently are estimated on the basis of sample statistics. A *parameter* is a summary value for a population or process, whereas a *sample statistic* is a summary value for a sample. In order to use a sample statistic as an estimator of a parameter, the sample must be a *random sample* from a population or a *rational subgroup* from a process.

A *point estimator* is the numeric value of a sample statistic that is used to estimate the value of a population or process parameter. One of the most important characteristics of an estimator is that it be unbiased. An *unbiased estimator* is a sample statistic whose expected value is equal to the parameter being estimated. An *expected value* is the long-run mean average of the sample statistic. The elimination of any systematic bias is assured when the sample statistic is for a *random sample* taken from a population or a *rational subgroup* taken from a process. Either sampling method assures that the sample is unbiased but does not eliminate sampling variability, or *sampling error*, as explained in the following section.

Table 8.1 presents some frequently used point estimators of population parameters. In every case, the appropriate estimator of a population

Population parameter	Estimator
Mean, μ	$\bar{X}$
Difference between the means of two populations, $\mu_1 - \mu_2$	$\bar{X}_1 - \bar{X}_2$
Proportion, π	$\hat{p}$
Difference between the proportions in two populations, $\pi_1 - \pi_2$	$\hat{p}_1 - \hat{p}_2$
Variance, σ^2	s^2
Standard deviation, σ	s

Table 8.1 Frequently used point estimators

parameter simply is the corresponding sample statistic. However, note that the formula in Chapter 4 for the sample variance includes a correction factor. Without this correction, the sample variance would be a biased estimator of the population variance.

The Concept of a Sampling Distribution

Your understanding of the concept of a sampling distribution is fundamental to your understanding of statistical inference. As we have already established, a *population distribution* is the distribution of all the individual measurements in a population, and a *sample distribution* is the distribution of the individual values included in a sample. In contrast to such distributions for individual measurements, a *sampling distribution* refers to the distribution of different values that a sample statistic, or estimator, would have over many samples of the same size. Thus, even though we typically would have just one random sample or rational subgroup, we recognize that the particular sample statistic that we determine, such as the sample mean or median, is not exactly equal to the respective population parameter. Further, *a sample statistic will vary in value from sample to sample* because of random sampling variability, or *sampling error*. This is the idea underlying the concept that any sample statistic is in fact a type of variable whose distribution of values is represented by a sampling distribution.

Sampling Distribution of the Mean

We now turn our attention specifically to the sampling distribution of the sample mean. When the mean of just one sample is used in statistical inference about a population mean, it would be useful to know the expected value and the variability to be expected from sample to sample. Amazingly, we are able to determine both the expected value and the variability of the sample mean by knowing the mean and standard deviation of the population (or process). But what if the parameter values are not known, and we have data from only one sample? Even then, the variability of the sample statistic, such as the sample mean, from sample to sample can still be determined and used in statistical inference.

The sampling distribution of the mean is described by determining the mean of such a distribution, which is the expected value $E(\overline{X})$, and the standard deviation of the distribution of sample means, designated $\sigma_{\overline{x}}$. Because this standard deviation is indicative of the accuracy of the sample statistic as an estimator of a population mean, it is usually called the *standard error of the mean*. When the population or process parameters are known, the expected value and standard error for the sampling distribution of the mean are:

$$E(\overline{X}) = \mu$$

$$\sigma_{\overline{x}} = \frac{\sigma}{\sqrt{n}}$$

When sampling from a population that is finite and of limited size, a *finite correction factor* is available for the correct determination of the standard error. The effect of this correction factor is always to reduce the value that otherwise would be calculated. As a general rule, the correction is negligible and can be omitted when $n < 0.05N$, that is, when the sample size is less than 5 percent of the population size. Because populations from which samples are taken are usually large, many texts and virtually all computer programs do not include this correction option. The formula for the standard error of the mean with the finite correction factor included is:

$$\sigma_{\overline{x}} = \frac{\sigma}{\sqrt{n}} \sqrt{\frac{N-n}{N-1}}$$

The correction factor in the above formula is the factor under the square root that has been appended to the basic formula for the standard error of the mean.

You Need to Know

This same correction factor can be appended to the formulas for any of the standard error formulas for the mean, difference between means, proportion, and difference between proportions that are described and used in this and the following chapters.

If the standard deviation of the population or process is not known, the standard error of the mean can be estimated by using the sample standard deviation as an estimator of the population standard deviation. To differentiate this estimated standard error from the precise one based on a known σ, it is designated by the symbol $s_{\bar{x}}$.

The Central Limit Theorem

If the population or process from which a sample is taken is normally distributed, then the sampling distribution of the mean also will be normally distributed, regardless of sample size. However, what if a population is not normally distributed? Remarkably, a theorem from mathematical statistics still permits application of the normal distribution with respect to such sampling distributions. The *central limit theorem* states that as sample size is increased, the sampling distribution of the mean approaches the normal distribution in form, *regardless of the form of the population distribution from which the sample was taken.* For practical purposes, the sampling distribution of the mean can be assumed to be approximately normally distributed, even for the most nonnormal populations or processes, whenever the sample size is $n \geq 30$. For populations that are only somewhat nonnormal, even a smaller sample size will suffice. But a sample size of at least 30 will take care of the most adverse population situation.

Determining Probability Values for the Sample Mean

If the sampling distribution of the mean is normally distributed, either because the population is normally distributed or because the central limit theorem is invoked, then we can determine probabilities regarding the possible values of the sample mean, given that the population mean and standard deviation are known. The process is analogous to determining probabilities for individual observations using the normal distribution. In the present application, however, it is the designated value of the *sample mean* that is converted into a value of z in order to uses the table of normal probabilities. This conversion formula uses the *standard error of the mean* because this is the standard deviation for the variable $\overline{X}$. Thus, the conversion formula is:

$$z = \frac{\overline{X} - \mu}{\sigma_{\overline{x}}}$$

Example 8.1 An auditor takes a random sample of size $n = 36$ from a population of 1,000 accounts receivable. The mean value of the accounts receivable for the population is $\mu = \$260.00$, with the population standard deviation $\sigma = \$45.00$. What is the probability that the sample mean will be less than $250.00?

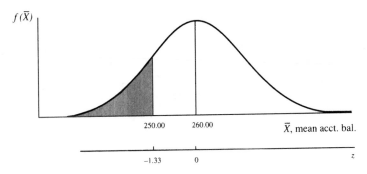

Figure 8-1

Figure 8-1 portrays the probability curve. The sampling distribution is described by the mean and standard error:

$$\mu = 260.00 \text{ (as given)}$$

$$\sigma_{\bar{x}} = \frac{45}{6} = 7.50$$

$$z = \frac{250.00 - 260.00}{7.50} = \frac{-10}{7.50} = -1.33.$$

Therefore,

$$P(\bar{X} < 250.00 \mid \mu = 260.00, \sigma_{\bar{x}} = 7.50) = P(z < -1.33)$$
$$P(z < -1.33) = 0.5000 - P(-1.33 \le z \le 0)$$
$$= 0.5000 - 0.4082 = 0.0918.$$

Confidence Intervals for the Mean Using the Normal Distribution

Example 8.1 above is concerned with determining the probability that the sample mean will have various values given that the population mean and standard deviation are known. What is involved is *deductive reasoning* with respect to the sample result based on known population parameters. We now concern ourselves with *inductive reasoning* by using sample data to make statements about the value of the population mean.

The methods of interval estimation in this section are based on the assumption that the normal probability distribution can be used. Such use is warranted whenever $n \ge 30$, because of the central limit theorem, or when $n < 30$ but the population is normally distributed and σ is known.

Although the sample mean is useful as an unbiased estimator of the population mean, there is no way of expressing the degree of accuracy of a point estimator. In fact, mathematically speaking, the probability that the sample mean is exactly correct as an estimator of the population mean is $P = 0$. A *confidence interval* for the mean is an estimate interval constructed with respect to the sample mean by which the likelihood that the interval includes the value of the population mean can be specified. The *level of confidence* associated with a confidence interval indicates the long-run percentage of such intervals that would include the parameter being estimated.

Confidence intervals for the mean typically are constructed with the unbiased estimator at the midpoint of the interval. When use of the normal probability distribution is warranted, the confidence interval for the mean is determined by:

$$\overline{X} \pm z\sigma_{\overline{x}}$$

or when the population σ is not known by:

$$\overline{X} \pm zs_{\overline{x}}$$

The most frequently used confidence intervals are the 90 percent, 95 percent, and 99 percent confidence intervals. The values of z required in conjunction with such intervals are given in Table 8.2.

z (the number of standard deviation units from the mean)	Proportion of area in the interval $\mu \pm z\sigma$
1.645	0.90
1.96	0.95
2.58	0.99

Table 8.2 Selected proportions of area under the normal curve

Determining the Required Sample Size for Estimating the Mean

Suppose that the desired size of a confidence interval and the level of confidence to be associated with it are specified. If σ is known or can be estimated, such as from the results of similar studies, the required sample size based on the use of the normal distribution is:

$$n = \left(\frac{z\sigma}{E} \right)^2$$

In the above formula, z is the value used for the specified level of confidence, σ is the standard deviation of the population, and E is the plus and minus sampling error allowed in the interval (always one-half the total confidence interval).

The *t* Distribution and Confidence Intervals for the Mean

Earlier in this chapter, we indicated that use of the normal distribution in estimating a population mean is warranted for any large sample, and for a small sample only if the population is normally distributed *and* σ is known. In this section we handle the situation in which the sample is small and the population is normally distributed, but σ is not known.

If a population is normally distributed, the sampling distribution of the mean for any sample size will also be normally distributed; this is true whether σ is known or not. However, in the process of inference each value of the mean is converted to a standard normal value, *and herein lies the problem*. If σ is unknown, the conversion formula includes a variable in the denominator, because s will be somewhat different from sample to sample. The result is that use of the variable $s_{\bar{x}}$ rather than the constant $\sigma_{\bar{x}}$ in the denominator results in converted values that are not distributed as z values. Instead, the values are distributed according to the t distribution, which is platykurtic as compared with the distribution of z. The distribution is a family of distributions, with a somewhat different distribution associated with the *degrees of freedom (df)*. For a confidence interval for the population mean based on a sample of size n, $df = n - 1$.

The degrees of freedom indicate the number of values that are in fact "free to vary" in the sample that serves as the basis for the confidence interval. Offhand, it would seem that all of the values in the sample are always free to vary in their measured values. However, what is different for the t distribution as compared to the z is that both the sample mean and the sample standard deviation are required as parameter estimators in order to define a confidence interval for the population mean. The need for the additional parameter estimate is a limitation on the sample. Without considering the mathematical abstractions, the bottom line is that, in general, one degree of freedom is lost with each additional parameter estimate that is required beyond the one parameter toward which the statistical inference is directed.

Use of the t distribution for inference concerning the population mean is appropriate whenever σ is not known and the sampling distribution of the mean is normal (either because the population is normally distributed or the central limit theorem is invoked). Just as is true for the z distribution, the t distribution has a mean of 0. However, it is flatter and wider than the z (and thus has a standard deviation > 1.0). With increasing sample size and df, the t distribution approaches the form of the standard normal z distribution. For hand calculations, a general rule is that required t values can be approximated by z values when $n > 30$ (or $df < 29$).

Summary Table for Interval Estimation of the Population Mean

Population	Sample size	σ known	σ unknown
Normally distributed	Large ($n \geq 30$)	$\bar{X} \pm z\sigma_{\bar{x}}$	$\bar{X} \pm ts_{\bar{x}}$ or $\bar{X} \pm zs_{\bar{x}}$**
	Small ($n < 30$)	$\bar{X} \pm z\sigma_{\bar{x}}$	$\bar{X} \pm ts_{\bar{x}}$
Not normally distributed	Large ($n \geq 30$)	$\bar{X} \pm z\sigma_{\bar{x}}$*	$\bar{X} \pm ts_{\bar{x}}$* or $\bar{X} \pm zs_{\bar{x}}$†
	Small ($n < 30$)	Nonparametric procedures directed toward the median generally would be used.	

* Central limit theorem is invoked.
** z is used as an approximation of t.
† Central limit theorem is invoked, and z is used as an approximation of t.

Table 8.3 Interval estimation of the population mean

Solved Problems

Solved Problem 8.1 For a particular brand of TV picture tube, it is known that the mean operating life of the tubes is $\mu = 9{,}000$ hr with a standard deviation of $\sigma = 500$ hr. (*a*) Determine the expected value and standard error of the sampling distribution of the mean given a sample size of $n = 25$. (*b*) Interpret the meaning of the computed values.

Solution: (*a*)
$$E(\overline{X}) = \mu = 9{,}000$$
$$\sigma_{\overline{x}} = 100$$

(*b*) These calculations indicate that in the long run the mean of a large group of samples means, each based on a sample size of $n = 25$, will be equal to 9,000 hr. Further, the variability of these sample means with respect to the expected value of 9,000 hr is expressed by a standard deviation of 100 hr.

Solved Problem 8.2 Suppose that the standard deviation of the tube life for a particular brand of TV picture tube is known to be $\sigma = 500$, but that the mean operating life is unknown. Overall, the operating life of the tubes is assumed to be approximately normally distributed. For a sample of $n = 15$, the mean operating life is $\overline{X} = 8{,}900$ hr. Determine the 95 percent confidence intervals for estimating the population mean.

Solution: The normal probability distribution can be used in this case because the population is normally distributed and σ is known.

$$\overline{X} \pm z\sigma_{\overline{x}} = 8{,}900 \pm 1.96 \frac{\sigma}{\sqrt{n}}$$
$$= 8{,}647 \text{ to } 9{,}153$$

Solved Problem 8.3 With respect to Solved Problem 8.2, suppose that the population can be assumed to be normally distributed, but that the population standard deviation is not known. Rather, the sample standard deviation $s = 500$ and $\overline{X} = 8{,}900$. Estimate the population mean using a 90 percent confidence interval.

Solution: Because $n \geq 30$ the normal distribution can be used as an approximation of the t distribution. However, because the population is normally distributed, the central limit theorem need not be invoked. Therefore,

$$\overline{X} \pm zs_{\bar{x}} = 8,900 \pm 1.645\left(\frac{500}{\sqrt{35}}\right) = 8,761 \; to \; 9,039 \; hr$$

Solved Problem 8.4 A prospective purchaser wishes to estimate the mean dollar amount of sales per customer at a toy store located at an airlines terminal. Based on the data from other similar airports, the standard deviation of such sales amounts is estimated to be about $\sigma = \$3.20$. What size of random sample should be collected, as a minimum, if the purchaser wants to estimate the mean sales amount within $\$1.00$ and with 99 percent confidence?

Solution: $n = (z\sigma/E)^2 = [(2.58)(3.20)/1.00]^2 = 68.16$

Solved Problem 8.5 Referring to Solved Problem 8.4, what is the minimum required sample size if the distribution of sales amounts is not assumed to be normal and the purchaser wishes to estimate the mean sales amount within $\$2.00$ with 99 percent confidence?

Solution: $n = (z\sigma/E)^2 = [(2.58)(3.20)/2.00]^2 = 17.04$

However, because the population is not assumed to be normally distributed, the minimum sample size is $n = 30$, so that the central limit theorem can be invoked as the basis for using the normal probability distribution for constructing the confidence interval.

Chapter 9
OTHER
CONFIDENCE
INTERVALS

IN THIS CHAPTER:

- ✔ *Confidence Intervals for the Difference between Two Means Using the Normal Distribution*
- ✔ *The t Distribution and Confidence Intervals for the Difference between Two Means*
- ✔ *Confidence Intervals for the Population Proportion*
- ✔ *Determining the Required Sample Size for Estimating the Proportion*
- ✔ *Confidence Intervals for the Difference between Two Proportions*
- ✔ *The Chi-Square Distribution and*

Confidence Intervals for the Variance and Standard Deviation
✔ *Solved Problems*

Confidence Intervals for the Difference between Two Means Using the Normal Distribution

There is often a need to estimate the difference between two population means, such as the difference between the wage levels in two firms. The confidence interval is constructed in a manner similar to that used for estimating the mean, except that the relevant standard error for the sampling distribution is the standard error of the difference between means. Use of the normal distribution is based on the same conditions as for the sampling distribution of the mean, except that two samples are involved. The formula used for estimating the difference between two population means with confidence intervals is:

$$(\overline{X}_1 - \overline{X}_2) \pm z\sigma_{\bar{x}_1 - \bar{x}_2} \quad or \quad (\overline{X}_1 - \overline{X}_2) \pm zs_{\bar{x}_1 - \bar{x}_2}$$

When the standard deviations of the two populations are known, the standard error of the difference between means is:

$$\sigma_{\bar{x}_1 - \bar{x}_2} = \sqrt{\sigma_{\bar{x}_1}^2 + \sigma_{\bar{x}_2}^2}$$

When the standard deviations of the populations are not known, the estimated standard error of the difference between means given that use of the normal distribution is appropriate is:

$$s_{\bar{x}_1 - \bar{x}_2} = \sqrt{s_{\bar{x}_1}^2 + s_{\bar{x}_2}^2}$$

Note!

In addition to the two-sided confidence interval, a one-sided confidence interval for the difference between means can also be constructed.

The *t* Distribution and Confidence Intervals for the Difference between Two Means

As explained in Chapter 8, use of the *t* distribution in conjunction with one sample is necessary when:

1. Population standard deviations σ are not known.
2. Samples are small ($n < 30$). If samples are large, then *t* values can be approximated by the standard normal *z*.
3. Populations are assumed to be approximately normally distributed.

   In addition to the above, when the *t* distribution is used to define confidence intervals for the difference between two means, rather than for inference concerning only one population mean, an additional assumption usually required is: the two populations variances are equal.

   Because of the above equality assumption, the first step in determining the standard error of the difference between means when the *t* distribution is to be used typically is to pool the two sample variances:

$$\hat{\sigma}^2 = \frac{(n_1 - 1)s_1^2 + (n_2 - 1)s_2^2}{n_1 + n_2 - 2}$$

   The standard error of the difference between means based on using the pooled variance estimate is:

$$\hat{\sigma}_{\bar{x}_1 - \bar{x}_2} = \sqrt{\frac{\hat{\sigma}^2}{n_1} + \frac{\hat{\sigma}^2}{n_2}}$$

Where $df = n_1 + n_2 - 2$, the confidence interval is:

$$(\overline{X}_1 - \overline{X}_2) \pm t_{df}\, \hat{\sigma}_{\overline{x}_1 - \overline{x}_2}$$

Note that in the two-sample case it is possible for each sample to be small, and yet the normal distribution could be used to approximate the t because $df \geq 29$. However, in such use the two populations must be assumed to be approximately normally distributed, because the central limit theorem cannot be invoked with respect to a small sample.

Confidence Intervals for the Population Proportion

The probability distribution that is applicable to proportions is the binomial probability distribution. However, the mathematics associated with determining a confidence interval for an unknown population proportion on the basis of the Bernoulli process is complex. Therefore, all applications-oriented textbooks utilize the normal distribution as an approximation of the exact solution for confidence dence intervals for proportions. However, when the population proportion p (or π) is not known, most statisticians suggest that a sample of $n \geq 100$ should be taken.

The variance of the distribution of proportions serves as the basis for the standard error. Given an observed sample proportion of $\hat{p}$, the estimated standard error of the proportion is:

$$s_{\hat{p}} = \sqrt{\frac{\hat{p}(1 - \hat{p})}{n}}$$

In the context of statistical estimation, the population p would not be known because that is the value being estimated. If the population is finite, then use of the finite correction factor is appropriate. As was the case for the standard error of the mean, use of this correction is generally not considered necessary if $n < 0.05N$. The approximate confidence interval for a population proportion is $\hat{p} \pm z s_{\hat{p}}$. In addition to the two-sided confidence interval, a one-sided confidence interval for the population proportion can also be determined.

Determining the Required Sample Size for Estimating the Proportion

Before a sample is actually collected, the minimum required sample size can be determined by specifying the level of confidence required, the sampling error that is acceptable, and by making an initial estimate of π, the unknown population proportion:

$$(\hat{p}_1 - \hat{p}_2) \pm z s_{\hat{p}_1 - \hat{p}_2}$$

Above, z is the value used for the specified confidence interval, π is the initial estimate of the population proportion, and E is the "plus and minus" sampling error allowed in the interval (always one-half the total confidence interval).

If an initial estimate of π is not possible, then it should be estimated as being 0.50. Such an estimate is conservative in that it is the value for which the largest sample size would be required. Under such an assumption, the general formula for sample size is simplified as follows: $n = (z/2E)^2$.

Confidence Intervals for the Difference between Two Proportions

In order to estimate the difference between the proportions in two populations, the unbiased point estimate of $(\pi_1 - \pi_2)$ is $(\hat{p}_1 - \hat{p}_2)$. The confidence interval involves use of the standard error of the difference between proportions. Use of the normal distribution is based on the same conditions as for the sampling distribution of the proportion, except that two samples are involved and the requirements apply to each of the two samples. The confidence interval for estimating the difference between two population proportions is:

$$(\hat{p}_1 - \hat{p}_2) \pm z s_{\hat{p}_1 - \hat{p}_2}$$

The standard error of the difference between proportions is determined by the formula below, wherein the value of each respective standard error of the proportion is calculated as described before:

$$s_{\hat{p}_1-\hat{p}_2} = \sqrt{s_{\hat{p}_1}^2 + s_{\hat{p}_2}^2}$$

The Chi-Square Distribution and Confidence Intervals for the Variance and Standard Deviation

Given a normally distributed population of values, the χ^2 (chi-square) distributions can be shown to be the appropriate probability distributions for the ratio $(n-1)s^2/\sigma^2$. There is a different chi-square distribution according to the value of $n-1$, which represents the degrees of freedom (df). Thus,

$$\chi_{df}^2 = \frac{(n-1)s^2}{\sigma^2}$$

Because the sample variance is the unbiased estimator of the population variance, the long-run expected value of the above ratio is equal to the degrees of freedom, or $n-1$. However, in any given sample the sample variance generally is not identical in value to the population variance. Since the ratio above is known to follow a chi-square distribution, this probability distribution can be used for statistical inference concerning an unknown variance or standard deviation.

Chi-square distributions are not symmetrical. Therefore, a two-sided confidence interval for a variance or standard deviation involves the use of two different chi square values, rather than the plus and minus approach used with the confidence intervals based on the normal and t distributions. The formula for constructing a confidence interval for the population variance is:

$$\frac{(n-1)s^2}{\chi_{df,upper}^2} \leq \sigma^2 \leq \frac{(n-1)s^2}{\chi_{df,lower}^2}$$

The confidence interval for the population standard deviation is:

$$\sqrt{\frac{(n-1)s^2}{\chi^2_{df,upper}}} \leq \sigma^2 \leq \sqrt{\frac{(n-1)s^2}{\chi^2_{df,lower}}}$$

Solved Problems

Solved Problem 9.1 A random sample of 50 households in community A has a mean household income of $\overline{X}$ = \$44,600 with a standard deviation s = \$2,200. A random sample of 50 households in community B has a mean of $\overline{X}$ = \$43,800 with a standard deviation of \$2,800. Estimate the difference in the average household income in the two communities using a 95 percent confidence interval.

Solution:

$$s_{\bar{x}_1} = s_1 / \sqrt{n_1} = \$311.17$$

$$s_{\bar{x}_2} = s_2 / \sqrt{n_2} = \$396.04$$

$$s_{\bar{x}_1 - \bar{x}_2} = \sqrt{s^2_{\bar{x}_1} + s_{\bar{x}_2}} = \$503.66$$

$$(\overline{X}_1 - \overline{X}_2) \pm zs_{\bar{x}_1 - \bar{x}_2} = 800 \pm 987.17 = -\$187.17 \text{ to } \$1,787.17$$

Solved Problem 9.2 For the income data reported in Solved Problem 9.1, estimate the maximum difference between the mean income levels in the first and second community by constructing a 95 percent lower confidence interval.

Solution:

$$\text{Est. } (\mu_1 - \mu_2) \leq 800 + 1.645(503.66) \leq \$1,628.52$$

Solved Problem 9.3 A college administrator collects data on a nationwide random sample of 230 students enrolled in M.B.A. programs and finds that 54 of these students have undergraduate degrees in business. Estimate the proportion of such students in the nationwide population who have undergraduate degrees in business, using a 90 percent confidence interval.

Solution:

$$\hat{p} = \frac{54}{230} = 0.235$$

$$s_{\hat{p}} = \sqrt{\frac{\hat{p}(1-\hat{p})}{n}} = 0.028$$

$$\hat{p} \pm z s_{\hat{p}} = 0.235 \pm 1.645(0.028)$$

$$= 0.235 \pm 0.046 \cong 0.19 \, to \, 0.28$$

Chapter 10
TESTING HYPOTHESES CONCERNING THE VALUE OF THE POPULATION MEAN

In This Chapter:

- ✔ *Introduction*
- ✔ *Basic Steps in Hypothesis Testing by the Critical Value Approach*
- ✔ *Testing a Hypothesis Concerning the Mean by Use of the Normal Distribution*
- ✔ *Type I and Type II Errors in Hypothesis Testing*
- ✔ *Determining the Required Sample Size for Testing the Mean*

✔ *Testing a Hypothesis Concerning the Mean by Use of the* t *Distribution*
✔ *The P-Value Approach to Testing Hypotheses Concerning the Population Mean*
✔ *The Confidence Interval Approach to Testing Hypotheses Concerning the Mean*
✔ *Testing with Respect to the Process Mean in Statistical Process Control*
✔ *Summary Table for Testing a Hypothesized Value of the Mean*
✔ *Solved Problems*

Introduction

The purpose of hypothesis testing is to determine whether a claimed (hypothesized) value for a population parameter, such as a population mean, should be accepted as being plausible based on sample evidence. Recall from Chapter 8 on sampling distributions that a sample mean generally will differ in value from the population mean. If the observed value of a sample statistic, such as the sample mean, is close to the claimed parameter value and differs only by an amount that would be  expected because of random sampling, then the hypothesized value is not rejected. If the sample statistic differs from the claim by an amount that cannot be ascribed to chance, then the hypothesis is rejected as not being plausible.

Three different procedures have been developed for testing hypotheses, with all of them leading to the same decision when the same probability (and risk) standards are used. In this chapter we first describe the *critical value approach* to hypothesis testing. By this approach, the so-called critical values of the test statistic that would dictate rejection of a hypothesis are determined, and then the observed test statistic is compared to the critical values. This is the first approach that was developed, and thus much of the language of hypothesis testing stems from it.

More recently, the *P-value approach* has become popular because it is the one most easily applied with computer software. This approach is based on determining the conditional probability that the observed value of a sample statistic could occur by chance, given that a particular claim for the value of the associated population parameter is in fact true. Finally, the *confidence interval approach* is based on observing whether the claimed value of a population parameter is included within the range of values that define a confidence interval for that parameter.

No matter which approach to hypothesis testing is used, note that if a hypothesized value is not rejected, and therefore is accepted, this does not constitute a "proof" that the hypothesized value is correct. Acceptance of a claimed value for the parameter simply indicates that it is a plausible value, based on the observed value of the sample statistic.

Basic Steps in Hypothesis Testing by the Critical Value Approach

Step 1. Formulate the null hypothesis and the alternative hypothesis. The *null hypothesis* (H_0) is the hypothesized parameter value that is compared with the sample result. It is rejected *only if* the sample result is unlikely to have occurred given the correctness of the hypothesis. The *alternative hypothesis* (H_1) is accepted only if the null hypothesis is rejected. The alternative hypothesis is also designated by (H_a) in many texts.

Step 2. Specify the level of significance to be used. The level of significance is the statistical standard that is specified for rejecting the null hypothesis. If a 5 percent level of significance is specified, then the null hypothesis is rejected only if the sample result is so different from the hypothesized value that a difference of that amount or larger would occur by chance with a probability of 0.05 or less.

Note that if the 5 percent level of significance is used, there is a probability of 0.05 of rejecting the null hypothesis when it is in fact true. This is called *Type I error*. The probability of Type I error is always equal to the level of significance that is used as the standard for rejecting the null hypothesis; it is designated by the lowercase Greek α (alpha), and thus α also designates the level of significance. The most frequently used levels of significance in hypothesis testing are the 5 percent and 1 percent levels.

A *Type II error* occurs if the null hypothesis is not rejected, and therefore accepted, when it is in fact false. Determining the probability of Type II error is explained later in this chapter. Table 10.1 summarizes the types of decisions and the possible consequences of the decisions which are made in hypothesis testing.

	Possible states	
Possible decision	Null hypothesis true	Null hypothesis false
Accept null hypothesis	Correctly accepted	Type II error
Reject null hypothesis	Type I error	Correctly rejected

Table 10.1 Consequences in decisions in hypothesis testing

Step 3. Select the test statistic. The test statistic will either be the sample statistic (the unbiased estimator of the parameter being tested), or a standardized version of the sample statistic. For example, in order to test a hypothesized value of the population mean, the mean of a random sample taken from that population could serve as the test statistic. However, if the sampling distribution of the mean is normally distributed, then the value of the sample mean typically is converted into a z value, which then serves as the test statistic.

Step 4. Establish the critical value or values of the test statistic. Having specified the null hypothesis, the level of significance, and the test statistic to be used, we now establish the critical value(s) of the test statistic. There may be one or two such values, depending on whether a so-called one-sided or two-sided test is involved. In either case, a *critical value* identifies the value of the test statistic that is required to reject the null hypothesis.

Step 5. Determine the actual value of the test statistic. For example, in testing a hypothesized value of the population mean, a random sample is collected and the value of sample mean is determined. If the critical value was established as a z value, then the sample mean is converted into a z value.

Step 6. Make a decision. The observed value of the sample statistic is compared with the critical value (or values) of the test statistic. The null hypothesis is then either rejected or not rejected. If the null hypothesis is rejected, the alternative hypothesis is accepted. In turn, this decision will have relevance to other decisions to be made by operating managers, such as whether a standard of performance is being maintained or which of two marketing strategies should be used.

Testing a Hypothesis Concerning the Mean by Use of the Normal Distribution

The normal probability distribution can be used for testing a hypothesized value of the population mean whenever $n \geq 30$, because of the central limit theorem, or when $n < 30$ but the population is normally distributed and σ is known.

A two-sided test is used when we are concerned about a possible deviation in *either* direction from the hypothesized value of the mean. The formula used to establish the critical values of the sample mean is similar to the formula for determining confidence limits for estimating the population mean, except that the hypothesized value of the population mean μ_0 is the reference point rather than the sample mean. The critical values of the sample mean for a two-sided test, according to whether or not σ is known, are:

$$\overline{X}_{CR} = \mu_0 \pm z\sigma_{\overline{X}}$$

or

$$\overline{X}_{CR} = \mu_0 \pm z s_{\overline{X}}$$

Instead of establishing critical values in terms of the sample mean, the critical values in hypothesis testing typically are specified in terms of z values. For the 5 percent level of significance the critical values z for a two-sided test are -1.96 and $+1.96$, for example. When the value of the sample mean is determined, it is converted to a z value so that it can be compared with the critical values of z. The conversion formula, according to whether or not σ is known, is:

$$z = \frac{\overline{X} - \mu_0}{\sigma_{\overline{X}}}$$

or

$$z = \frac{\overline{X} - \mu_0}{s_{\overline{X}}}$$

A *one-sided* test is appropriate when we are concerned about possible deviations in only one direction from the hypothesized value of the mean.

There is only one region of rejection for a one-sided test. The region of rejection for a one-sided test is always in the tail that represents support of the *alternative* hypothesis. As is the case for a two-sided test, the critical value can be determined for the mean, as such, or in terms of a z value. However, critical values for one-sided tests differ from those for two-sided tests because the given proportion of area is all in one tail of the distribution. Table 10.2 presents the values of z needed for one-sided and two-sided tests. The general formula to establish the critical value of the sample mean for a one-sided test, according to whether or not σ is known, is the same as the two-sided test.

Level of significance	Type of test	
	One-sided	Two-sided
5%	+1.645 (or −1.645)	±1.96
1%	+2.33 (or −2.33)	±2.58

Table 10.2 Critical values of z in hypothesis testing

Type I and Type II Errors in Hypothesis Testing

In this section Type I and Type II errors are considered entirely with respect to one-sided testing of a hypothesized mean. However, the basic concepts illustrated here apply to other hypothesis testing models as well.

The maximum probability of Type I error is designated by the Greek α (alpha). It is always equal to the level of significance used in testing the null hypothesis. This is so because by definition the proportion of area in the region of rejection is equal to the proportion of sample results that would occur in that region given that the null hypothesis is true.

The probability of Type II error is generally designated by the Greek β (beta). The only way it can be determined is with respect to a *specific* value included within the range of the *alternative* hypothesis.

With the level of significance and sample size held constant, the probability of Type II error decreases as the specific alternative value of the mean is set farther from the value in the null hypothesis. It increases as the alternative value is set closer to the value in the null hypothesis. An *operating characteristic (OC) curve* por- trays the probability of accepting the null hypothesis given various alternative values of the population mean. Figure 10-1 is the OC curve applicable to any *lower-tail test* for a hypothesized mean carried out at the 5 percent level of significance and based on the use of the normal probability distribution. Note that it is applicable to *any* such test, because the values on the horizontal axis are stated in units of the

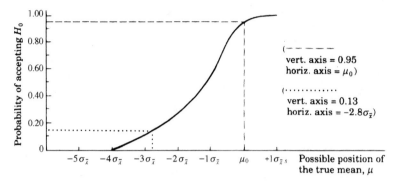

Figure 10-1

standard error of the mean. For any values to the left of μ_0, the probability of acceptance indicates the probability of Type II error. To the right of μ_0, the probabilities indicate correct acceptance of the null hypothesis. As indicated by the dashed lines, when $\mu = \mu_0$, the probability of accepting the null hypothesis is $1 - \alpha$.

In hypothesis testing, the concept of *power* refers to the probability of rejecting a null hypothesis that is false, given a specific alternative value of the parameter. Where the probability of Type II error is designated β, it follows that the power of the test is always $1 - \beta$. Referring to Figure 10-1, note that the power for alternative values of the mean is the difference between the value indicated by the *OC* curve and 1.0, and thus a *power curve* can be obtained by subtraction, with reference to the *OC* curve.

Determining the Required Sample Size for Testing the Mean

Before a sample is actually collected, the required sample size can be determined by specifying:

1. The hypothesized value of the mean
2. A specific alternative value of the mean such that the difference from the null hypothesized value is considered important
3. The level of significance to be used in the test

4. The probability of Type II error which is to be permitted
5. The value of the population standard deviation σ.

The formula for determining the minimum sample size required in conjunction with testing a hypothesized value of the mean, based on use of the normal distribution, is:

$$n = \frac{(z_0 - z_1)^2 \sigma^2}{(\mu_1 - \mu_0)^2}$$

In the above formula, z_0 is the critical value of z used in conjunction with the specified level of significance (α level). The value of σ either must be known or be estimated. The formula can be used for either one-sided or two-sided tests. The only value that differs for the two types of tests is the value of z_0 which is used.

Testing a Hypothesis Concerning the Mean by Use of the *t* Distribution

The *t* distribution is the appropriate basis for determining the standardized test statistic when the sampling distribution of the mean is normally distributed but σ is not known. The sampling distribution can be assumed to be normal either because the population is normal or because the sample is large enough to invoke the central limit theorem. The *t* distribution is required when the sample is small ($n < 30$). For larger samples, normal approximation can be used. For the critical value approach, the procedure is identical to that described for the normal distribution, except for the use of *t* instead of *z* as the test statistic. The test statistic is:

$$t = \frac{\overline{X} - \mu_0}{s_{\overline{X}}}$$

The *P*-Value Approach to Testing Hypotheses Concerning the Population Mean

The probability of the observed sample result occurring, given that the null hypothesis is true, is determined by the *P*-value approach, and this probability is then compared to the designated level of significance α.

Consistent with the critical value approach we described in the preceding sections, the idea is that a low *P* value indicates that the sample would be unlikely to occur when the null hypothesis is true; therefore, obtaining a low *P* value leads to rejection of the null hypothesis. Note that the *P* value is *not* the probability that the null hypothesis is true given the sample result. Rather, it is the probability of the sample result given that the null hypothesis is true.

For two-sided tests, the *P* value for the smaller tail of the distribution is determined, and then *doubled*. The resulting value indicates the probability of the observed amount of difference in *either* direction between the values of the sample mean and the hypothesized population mean.

The *P*-value approach has become popular because the standard format of computer output for hypothesis testing includes *P* values. The reader of the output determines whether a null hypothesis is rejected by comparing the reported *P* value with the desired level of significance.

 **Note!**

When hand calculation of probabilities based on the use of the *t* distribution is required, an exact *P* value cannot be determined because of the limitations of the standard table. However, no such limitations exist when using computer software.

The Confidence Interval Approach to Testing Hypotheses Concerning the Mean

By this approach, a confidence interval for the population mean is constructed based on the sample results, and then we observe whether the hypothesized value of the population mean is included within the confidence interval. If the hypothesized value is included within the interval, then the null hypothesis cannot be rejected. If the hypothesized value is not included in the interval, then the null hypothesis is rejected. Where α is the level of significance to be used for the test, the $1 - \alpha$ confidence interval is constructed.

For a one-tail test, a one-sided confidence interval is appropriate. However a simpler approach is to determine a two-sided interval, but at the level of confidence that would include the desired area in the one tail of interest. Specifically, for a one-sided test at $\alpha = 0.05$, the 90 percent, two-sided confidence interval is appropriate because this interval includes the are of 0.05 in the one tail of interest.

The confidence interval approach is favored in texts that emphasize the so-called *data-analysis* approach to business statistics. In the area of statistical description, the data-analysis approach gives special attention to *exploratory data analysis*. In the area of statistical inference, the philosophy of the data-analysis approach is that managers are more concerned with estimation and confidence intervals concerning unknown parameters, such as the uncertain level of sales for a new product, rather than in the concepts of hypothesis testing.

Testing with Respect to the Process Mean in Statistical Process Control

The use and interpretation of control charts in statistical process control is a direct application of the methods and concepts of hypothesis testing. The null hypothesis is that the process is *stable* and only common causes of variation exist. The alternative hypothesis is that the process is *unstable* and includes assignable-cause variation. The critical value approach to hypothesis testing is used, with the norm being that the lower and upper control limits (which are the same as "critical values" in the present chapter) are defined at ± 3 standard error units from the hypothesized mean for the process.

Summary Table for Testing a Hypothesized Value of the Mean

Population	Sample size	σ known	σ unknown
Normally distributed	Large ($n \geq 30$)	$z = \dfrac{\bar{X} - \mu_0}{\sigma_{\bar{x}}}$	$t = \dfrac{\bar{X} - \mu_0}{s_{\bar{x}}}$ or $z = \dfrac{\bar{X} - \mu_0}{s_{\bar{x}}}$**
	Small ($n < 30$)	$z = \dfrac{\bar{X} - \mu_0}{\sigma_{\bar{x}}}$	$t = \dfrac{\bar{X} - \mu_0}{s_{\bar{x}}}$
Not normally distributed	Large ($n \geq 30$)	$z = \dfrac{\bar{X} - \mu_0}{\sigma_{\bar{x}}}$*	$t = \dfrac{\bar{X} - \mu_0}{s_{\bar{x}}}$* or $z = \dfrac{\bar{X} - \mu_0}{s_{\bar{x}}}$†
	Small ($n < 30$)	Nonparametric tests directed toward the median generally would be used.	

* Central limit theorem is invoked.
** z is used as an approximation of t.
† Central limit theorem is invoked and z is used as an approximation of t.

Table 10.3 Testing a hypothesized value of the mean

Solved Problems

Solved Problem 10.1 A representative of a community group informs the prospective developer of a shopping center that the average income per household in the area is $45,000. Suppose that for the type of area involved household income can be assumed to be approximately normally distributed, and that the standard deviation can be accepted as being equal to $\sigma = \$2,000$, based on an earlier study. For a random sample of $n = 15$ households, the mean household income is found to be $\overline{X} = \$44,000$. Test the null hypothesis that $\mu = \$45,000$ by establishing critical limits of the sample mean in terms of dollars, using the 5 percent level of significance.

Solution: Since $H_0: \mu = \$45,000$ and $H_1: \mu \neq \$45,000$, the critical limits of $\overline{X} (\alpha = 0.05)$ are:

$$\overline{X}_{CR} = 45,000 \pm 1.96(516.80) = \$43,987 \, and \, \$46,013$$

Since the sample mean of $\overline{X} = \$44,000$ is between the two critical limits and in the region of acceptance of the null hypothesis, the community representative's claim cannot be rejected at the 5 percent level of significance.

Solved Problem 10.2 Test the hypothesis in Solved Problem 10.1 by using the standard normal variable z as the test statistic.

Solution: $H_0: \mu = \$45,000$ and $H_1: \mu \neq \$45,000$
Critical $z (\alpha = 0.05) = \pm 1.96$
$\sigma_{\overline{x}} = \$516.80$
$z = -1.93$

Since the computed z of -1.93 is in the region of acceptance of the null hypothesis, the community representative's claim cannot be rejected at the 5 percent level of significance.

Solved Problem 10.3 With reference to the first two problems, the prospective developer is not really concerned about the possibility that the average household income is higher than the claimed $45,000, but only that it might be lower. Accordingly, reformulate the null and alternate hypotheses and carry out the appropriate statistical test, still giving the benefit of the doubt to the community representative's claim.

Solution: $H_0 : \mu = \$45,000$ and $H_1 : \mu < \$45,000$
Critical z ($\alpha = 0.05$) $= -1.645$
$s_{\bar{x}} = \$364.96$
$z = -1.93$

Since the computed z is less than the critical value, the null hypothesis is rejected, and the alternative hypothesis that the mean is less than $45,000 is accepted.

Solved Problem 10.4 For Solved Problem 10.3, suppose that the population standard deviation is not known, which typically would be the case, and the population of income figures is not assumed to be normally distributed. For a sample of $n = 30$ households, the sample standard deviation is $s = \$2,000$ and the sample mean remains $\bar{X} = \$44,000$. Test the null hypothesis that the mean household income in the population is at least $45,000, using the 5 percent level of significance.

Solution: $H_0 : \mu = \$45,000$ and $H_1 : \mu < \$45,000$
Critical z ($\alpha = 0.05$) $= -1.645$
$s_{\bar{x}} = \$364.96$
$z = -2.74$

Since the computed z is less than the critical value, the null hypothesis is rejected , and the alternative hypothesis that the mean is less than $45,000 is accepted. Notice that the computed value of z in this case is arithmetically smaller in value and more clearly in the region of rejection as compared with Solved Problem 10.3. This is due entirely to the increase in sample size, which results in a smaller value for the standard error of the mean.

Chapter 11
TESTING OTHER HYPOTHESES

IN THIS CHAPTER:

- ✔ Testing the Difference between Two Means Using the Normal Distribution
- ✔ Testing the Difference between Means Based on Paired Observations
- ✔ Testing a Hypothesis Concerning the Value of the Population Proportion
- ✔ Determining Required Sample Size for Testing the Proportion
- ✔ Testing with Respect to the Process Proportion in Statistical Process Control
- ✔ Testing the Difference between Two Population Proportions

Testing the Difference between Two Means Using the Normal Distribution

The procedure associated with testing a hypothesis concerning the difference between two population means is similar to that for testing a hypothesis concerning the value of one population mean. The procedure differs only in that the standard error of the difference between the means is used to determine the z (or t) value associated with the sample result. Use of the normal distribution is based on the same conditions as in the one-sample case, except that two independent random samples are involved. The general formula for determining the z value for testing a hypothesis concerning the difference between two means, according to whether the σ values for the two populations are known is:

$$z = \frac{(\overline{X}_1 - \overline{X}_2) - (\mu_1 - \mu_2)_0}{\sigma_{\overline{X}_1 - \overline{X}_2}}$$

or

$$z = \frac{(\overline{X}_1 - \overline{X}_2) - (\mu_1 - \mu_2)_0}{s_{\overline{X}_1 - \overline{X}_2}}$$

As implied by the above formulas, we may begin with any particular hypothesized difference, $(\mu_1 - \mu_2)_0$, that is to be tested. However, the usual null hypothesis is that the two samples have been obtained from populations with means that are equal. In this case, $(\mu_1 - \mu_2)_0 = 0$, and the above formulas are simplified as follows:

$$z = \frac{\overline{X}_1 - \overline{X}_2}{\sigma_{\overline{X}_1 - \overline{X}_2}}$$

or

$$z = \frac{\overline{X}_1 - \overline{X}_2}{s_{\overline{X}_1 - \overline{X}_2}}$$

In general, the standard error of difference between means is computed as described in Chapter 9. However, in testing the difference between two means, the null hypothesis of interest is generally not only that the sample means were obtained from populations with equal means, but that the two samples were in fact obtained from the same population of values. This means that $\sigma_1 = \sigma_2$, which we can simply designate σ. The assumed common variance is often estimated by pooling the two samples variances, and the estimated value of σ^2 is then used as the basis for the standard error of the difference. The pooled estimate of the population variance is:

$$\hat{\sigma}^2 = \frac{(n_1 - 1)s_1^2 + (n_2 - 1)s_2^2}{n_1 + n_2 - 2}$$

The estimated standard error of the difference based on the assumption that the population standard deviations are equal is:

$$\hat{\sigma}_{\overline{X}_1 - \overline{X}_2} = \sqrt{\frac{\hat{\sigma}^2}{n_1} + \frac{\hat{\sigma}^2}{n_2}}$$

The assumption that the two sample variances were obtained from populations with equal variances can itself be tested as the null hypothesis.

You Need to Know

When the difference between two means is tested by the use of the *t* distribution, a necessary assumption in the standard procedure used in most texts is that the variances of the two populations are equal.

Testing the Difference between Means Based on Paired Observations

The procedures in the previous sections are based on the assumption that the two samples were collected as two independent random samples. However, in many situations the samples are collected as pairs of values, such as when determining the productivity level of each worker before and after a training program. These are referred to as *paired observations*, or *matched pairs*. Also, as contrasted to independent samples, two samples that contain paired observations often are called *dependent samples*.

For paired observations the appropriate approach for testing the difference between the means of the two samples is to first determine the difference *d* between each pair of values, and then test the null hypothesis that the mean population *difference* is zero. Thus, from the computational standpoint the test is applied to the *one* sample of *d* values, with $H_0 : \mu_d = 0$.

The mean and standard deviation of the sample *d* values are obtained by use of the basic formulas, except that *d* is substituted for *X*. The mean difference for a set of differences between paired observations is:

$$\bar{d} = \frac{\Sigma d}{n}$$

The deviations formula and the computational formula for the standard deviation of the differences between paired observations are, respectively,

$$s_d = \sqrt{\frac{\Sigma(d - \bar{d})^2}{n-1}}$$

$$s_d = \sqrt{\frac{\Sigma d^2 - n\bar{d}^2}{n-1}}$$

The standard error of the mean difference between paired observations is obtained by the formula for the standard error of the mean, except that d is again substituted for X:

$$s_{\bar{d}} = \frac{s_d}{\sqrt{n}}$$

Because the standard error of the mean difference is computed on the basis of the standard deviation of the sample of differences (that is, the population value σ_d is unknown) and because values of d generally can be assumed to be normally distributed, the t distribution is appropriate for testing the null hypothesis that $\mu_d = 0$.

The degrees of freedom is the number of differences minus one, or $n - 1$. The standard normal z distribution can be used as an approximation of the t distributions when $n \geq 30$. The test statistic used to test the hypothesis that there is no difference between the means of a set of paired observations is:

$$t = \bar{d} / s_{\bar{d}}$$

Testing a Hypothesis Concerning the Value of the Population Proportion

The normal distribution can be used as an approximation of a binomial distribution when $n \geq 30$ and both $np \geq 5$ and $n(q) \geq 5$, where $q = 1 - p$. This is the basis upon which confidence intervals for the proportion are determined, where the standard error of the proportion is also discussed. However, in the

case of confidence intervals, a sample size of at least $n = 100$ is generally required.

In determining confidence intervals, the sample proportion $\hat{p}$ serves as the basis for the standard error. In hypothesis testing, the value of the standard error of the proportion generally is based on using the hypothesized value π_0:

$$\sigma_{\hat{p}} = \sqrt{\frac{\pi_0(1-\pi_0)}{n}}$$

The procedure associated with testing a hypothesized value of the proportion is identical to that described in Chapter 10, except that the null hypothesis is concerned with a value of the population proportion rather than the population mean. Thus, the formula for the z statistic for testing a hypothesis concerning the value of the population proportion is:

$$z = \frac{\hat{p} - \pi_0}{\sigma_{\hat{p}}}$$

Determining Required Sample Size for Testing the Proportion

Before a sample is actually collected, the required sample size for testing a hypothesis concerning the population proportion can be determined by specifying:

1. The hypothesized value of the proportion
2. A specific alternative value of the proportion such that the difference from the null hypothesized value is considered important
3. The level of significance to be used in the test
4. The probability of Type II error which is to be permitted.

The formula for determining the minimum sample size required for testing a hypothesized value of the proportion is:

$$n = \left[\frac{z_0\sqrt{\pi_0(1-\pi_0)} - z_1\sqrt{\pi_1(1-\pi_1)}}{\pi_1 - \pi_0} \right]^2$$

In the above formula, z_0 is the critical value of z used in conjunction with the specified level of significance (α level) while z_1 is the value of z with respect to the designated probability of Type II error (β level). On determining sample size for testing the mean, z_0 and z_1 always have opposite algebraic signs. The result is that two products in the numerator will always be accumulated. Also, the formula can be used in conjunction with either one-tail or two-tail tests and any fractional sample size is rounded up. Finally, the sample size should be large enough to warrant use of the normal probability distribution in conjunction with π_0 and π_1.

Testing with Respect to the Process Proportion in Statistical Process Control

The use and interpretation of control charts in statistical process control is a direct application of the methods and concepts of hypothesis testing. The control limits for a process proportion are defined at ± 3 standard error units for the hypothesized (acceptable) value.

Testing the Difference between Two Population Proportions

When we wish to test the hypothesis that the proportions in two populations are not different, the two sample proportions are pooled as a basis for determining the standard error of the difference between proportions. The pooled estimate of the population proportion, based on the proportions obtained in two independent samples, is:

$$\hat{\pi} = \frac{n_1 \hat{p}_1 + n_2 \hat{p}_2}{n_1 - n_2}$$

The standard error of the difference between proportions used in conjunction with testing the assumption of no difference is:

$$\hat{\sigma}_{\hat{p}_1 - \hat{p}_2} = \sqrt{\frac{\hat{\pi}(1-\hat{\pi})}{n_1} + \frac{\hat{\pi}(1-\hat{\pi})}{n_2}}$$

The formula for the z statistic for testing the null hypothesis that there in no difference between two population proportions is:

$$z = \frac{\hat{p}_1 - \hat{p}_2}{\hat{\sigma}_{\hat{p}_1 - \hat{p}_2}}$$

A test of the difference between proportions can be carried out as either a one-sided test or a two-sided test.

Testing a Hypothesized Value of the Variance Using the Chi-Square Distribution

For a normally distributed population the ratio $(n-1)s^2/\sigma^2$ follows a χ^2 probability distribution, with there being a different chi-square distribution according to degrees of freedom $(n-1)$. Therefore, the statistic that is used to test a hypothesis concerning the value of the population variance is:

$$\chi^2 = \frac{(n-1)s^2}{\sigma_0^2}$$

The test based on the above formula can be either a one-sided test or a two-sided test, although most often hypotheses about a population variance relate to one-sided tests.

Testing with Respect to Process Variability in Statistical Process Control

The use and interpretation of control charts in statistical process control is a direct application of methods and concepts of hypothesis testing. Process variability is monitored and controlled either with respect to the process *standard deviation* or the process *range*. As is the case with control charts for the process mean and process proportion, the control limits are defined at ± 3 standard error units with respect to the expected centerline value on the chart when the null hypothesis that there is no assignable-cause variation is true.

The *F* Distribution and Testing the Equality of Two Population Variances

The *F* distribution can be shown to be the appropriate probability model for the ratio of the variances of two samples taken independently from the same normally distributed population, with there being a difference *F* distribution for every combination of the degrees of freedom *df* associated with each sample. For each sample, $df = n - 1$. The statistic that is used to test the null hypothesis that two population variances are equal is:

$$F_{df_1, df_2} = \frac{s_1^2}{s_2^2}$$

Since each sample variance is an unbiased estimator of the same population variance, the long-run expected value of the above ratio is about 1.0. However, for any given pair of samples the sample variances are not likely to be identical in value, even though the null hypothesis is true. Since this ratio is known to follow an *F* distribution, this probability distribution can be used in conjunction with testing the difference between two variances. Although a necessary mathematical assumption is that the two populations are normally distributed, the *F* test has been demonstrated to be relatively robust and insensitive to departures from normality when each population is unimodal and the sample sizes are about equal.

Alternative Approaches to Testing the Null Hypothesis

The *P*-value approach and the confidence interval approach are alternatives to the critical value approach to hypothesis testing used in the preceding sections of this chapter.

By the *P*-value approach, instead of comparing the observed value of a test statistic with a critical value, the probability of the occurrence of the test statistic, given that the null hypothesis is true, is determined and compared to the level of significance α. The null hypothesis is rejected if the *P* value is less then the designated α.

By the confidence interval approach, the $1 - \alpha$ confidence interval is constructed for the parameter value of concern. If the hypothesized value of the parameter is not included in the interval, then the null hypothesis is rejected.

Solved Problems

Solved Problem 11.1 A random sample of $n_1 = 12$ students majoring in accounting in a college of business has a mean grade-point average of 2.70 (where A = 4.0) with a sample standard deviation of 0.40. For the students majoring in computer information systems, a random sample of $n_2 = 10$ students has a mean grade-point average of 2.90 with a standard deviation of 0.30. The grade-point values are assumed to be normally distributed. Test the null hypothesis that the mean-grade point average for the two categories of students is not different, using the 5 percent level of significance.

Solution: $H_0 : (\mu_1 - \mu_2) = 0, H_1: (\mu_1 - \mu_2) = 0, X_1 = 2.70, X_2 = 2.90, s_1 = 0.40, s_2 = 0.30, n_1 = 12, n_2 = 10,$
Critical t $(df = 20, \alpha = 0.05) = \pm 2.086$
$t = -1.290$
The calculated value of $t = -1.290$ is in the region of acceptance of the null hypothesis. Therefore the null hypothesis that there is no difference between the grade-point averages cannot be rejected.

Solved Problem 11.2 A company training director wishes to compare a new approach to technical training, involving a combination of tutorial computer disks and laboratory problem solving, with the traditional lecture-discussion approach. Twelve pairs of trainees are matched according to prior background and academic performance, and one member of each pair is assigned to the traditional class and the other to the new approach. At the end of the course, the level of learning is determined by an examination covering basic information as well as the ability to apply the information. Because the training director wishes to give the benefit of the doubt to the established instructional system, the null hypothesis is formulated that the mean performance for the established system is equal to or greater than the mean level of performance for the new system. Test this hypothesis at the 5 percent level of significance. The sample performance data are presented in the first three columns of Table 11.1

Trainee pair	Traditional method (X_1)	New approach (X_2)	d ($X_1 - X_2$)	d^2
1	89	94	−5	25
2	87	91	−4	16
3	70	68	2	4
4	83	88	−5	25
5	67	75	−8	64
6	71	66	5	25
7	92	94	−2	4
8	81	88	−7	49
9	97	96	1	1
10	78	88	−10	100
11	94	95	−1	1
12	79	87	−8	64
Total	988	1,030	−42	378

Table 11.1 Training program data and worksheet for computing the mean difference and the standard deviation of the difference

Solution:

Mean performance (traditional method) = (988/12) = 82.33

Mean performance (new approach) = (1030/12) = 85.83

$H_0 : \mu_d = 0 \quad H_1 : \mu_d < 0$

Critical t ($df = 11$, $\alpha = 0.05$) = −1.796

$$\bar{d} = \frac{\Sigma d}{n} = \frac{-42}{12} = -3.5$$

$$s_d = 4.58$$

$$s_{\bar{d}} = \frac{s_d}{\sqrt{n}} = \frac{4.58}{\sqrt{12}} = 1.32$$

$$t = \frac{\bar{d}}{s_{\bar{d}}} = \frac{-3.5}{1.32} = -2.652$$

The computed value of t of −2.652 is less than the critical value of −1.796 for this lower tail-test. Therefore the null hypothesis is rejected at the 5 percent level of significance, and we conclude that the mean level of performance for those trained by the new approach is superior to those trained by the traditional method.

Solved Problem 11.3 It is hypothesized that no more than 5 percent of the parts being produced in a manufacturing process are defective. For a random sample of $n = 100$ parts, 10 are found to be defective. Test the null hypothesis at the 5 percent level of significance.

Solution:
$H_0 : \pi = 0.05 \qquad H_1 : \pi > 0.05$
Critical z ($\alpha = 0.05$) = +1.645
(Use of the normal distribution is warranted because $n \geq 30$, $n\pi_0 \geq 5$, and $n(1 - \pi_0) \geq 5$.)

$$\sigma_{\hat{p}} = \sqrt{\frac{\pi_0(1 - \pi_0)}{n}} = \sqrt{\frac{(0.05)(0.95)}{100}} = 0.022$$

$$z = \frac{\hat{p} - \pi_0}{\sigma_{\hat{p}}} = \frac{0.10 - 0.05}{0.022} = +2.27$$

The calculated value of z of +2.27 is greater than the critical value of +1.645 for this upper-tail test. Therefore with 10 parts out of 100 found to be defective, the hypothesis that the proportion defective in the population is at or below 0.05 is rejected, using the 5 percent level of significance in the test.

Chapter 12
THE CHI-SQUARE TEST FOR THE ANALYSIS OF QUALITATIVE DATA

IN THIS CHAPTER:

✔ *General Purpose of the Chi-Square Test*
✔ *Goodness of Fit Tests*
✔ *Tests for the Independence of Two Categorical Variables (Contingency Table Tests)*
✔ *Testing Hypotheses Concerning Proportions*
✔ *Solved Problems*

General Purpose of the Chi-Square Test

The procedures that are described in this chapter all involve the comparison of the observed pattern of the frequencies of observations for sample data have been entered into defined data categories, with the expected pattern of frequencies based on a particular null hypothesis.

Use of the χ^2 (chi-square) probability distribution with respect to statistical inference concerning the population variance is described in Chapters 9 and 11. The test statistic presented in the following sections also is distributed as the chi-square probability model, and since hypothesis testing is involved, the basic steps in hypothesis testing described in Chapter 10 apply in this chapter as well.

This chapter covers the use of the chi-square test for testing the *goodness of fit*, testing the *independence of two variables*, and testing *hypotheses concerning proportions*. One of the tests of proportions is that of testing the *differences among several population proportions*, which is an extension of testing the difference between two population proportions.

Goodness of Fit Tests

The null hypothesis in a goodness of fit test is a stipulation concerning the expected pattern of frequencies in a set of categories. The expected pattern may conform to the assumption of equal likelihood and may therefore be uniform, or the expected pattern may conform to such patterns as the binomial, Poisson, or normal.

For the null hypothesis to be accepted, the differences between observed and expected frequencies must be attributable to sampling variability at the designated level of significance. Thus, the chi-square test statistic is based on the magnitude of this difference for each category in the frequency distribution. The chi-square value for testing the difference between obtained and expected patterns of frequencies is:

$$\chi^2 = \Sigma \frac{(f_0 - f_e)^2}{f_e}$$

By the above formula, note that if the observed frequencies are very close to the expected frequencies, then the calculated value of the chi-square statistic will be close to zero. As the observed frequencies become increasingly different from the expected frequencies, the value of chi-square becomes larger. Therefore it follows that the chi-square test involves the use of just the *upper tail* of the chi-square distribution to determine whether an observed pattern of frequencies is different from an expected pattern.

The required value of the chi-square test statistic to reject the null hypothesis depends on the level of significance that is specified and the degrees of freedom. In goodness of fit tests, the degrees of freedom df are equal to the number of categories minus the number of parameter estimators based on the sample and minus 1. Where k = number of categories of data and m = number of parameter values estimated on the basis of the sample, the degrees of freedom in a chi-square goodness of fit test are $df = k - m - 1$.

When the null hypothesis is that the frequencies are equally distributed, no parameter estimation is ever involved and $m = 0$. The subtraction of 1 is always included, because given a total number of observations, once observed frequencies have been entered in $k - 1$ categories of a table of frequencies, the last cell is in fact not free to vary.

Computed values of the chi-square test statistic are based on discrete counts, whereas the chi-square distribution is a continuous distribution. When the expected frequencies f_e for the cells are not small, this factor is not important in terms of the extent to which the distribution of the test statistic is approximated by the chi-square distribution. *A frequently used rule is that the expected frequency f_e for each cell, or category, should be at least 5.* Cells that do not meet this criterion should be combined with adjacent categories, when possible, so that this requirement is satisfied. The reduced number of categories then becomes the basis for determining the degrees of freedom df applicable in the test situation.

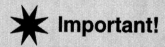

★ Important!

The expected frequencies for all cells of a data table also can be increased by increasing the overall sample size.

The expected frequencies may be based on any hypothesis regarding the form of the population frequency distribution, if the hypothesis is based on the observed historical pattern of frequencies, then, as in the case of the equally likely hypothesis, no parameter estimation is involved, and $df = k - m - 1 = k - 0 - 1 = k - 1$.

Tests for the Independence of Two Categorical Variables (Contingency Table Tests)

In the case of goodness of fit tests there is only one categorical variable, such as the screen size of TV sets which have been sold, and what is tested is a hypothesis concerning the pattern of frequencies, or the distribution, of the variable. The observed frequencies can be listed as a single row, or as a single column, of categories. *Tests for independence* involve (at least) two categorical variables, and what is tested is the assumption that the variables are statistically independent. Independence implies that knowledge of the category in which an observation is classified with respect to one variable has no affect on the probability of the other variable being in one of the several categories. When two variables are involved, the observed frequencies are entered in a two-way classification table, or *contingency table*. The dimensions of such tables are defined by $r \times k$, in which r indicates the number of rows and k indicates the number of columns.

If the null hypothesis of independence is rejected for classified data, this indicates that the two variables are *dependent* and that there is a *relationship* between them.

Given the hypothesis of independence of the two variables, the expected frequency associated with each cell of a contingency table should be proportionate to the total observed frequencies included in the column and in the row in which the cell is located as related to the total sample size. Where f_r is the total frequency in a given row and f_k is the total frequency in a given column, a convenient formula for determining the expected frequency for the cell of the contingency table that is located in that row and column is:

$$f_e = \frac{f_r f_k}{n}$$

The general formula for the degrees of freedom associated with a test for independence is: $df = (r - 1)(k - 1)$.

Testing Hypotheses Concerning Proportions

Testing a Hypothesized Value of the Proportion

Given a hypothesized population proportion and an observed proportion for a random sample taken from the population, in Chapter 11 we used the normal probability distribution as an approximation for the binomial process in order to test the null hypothesis. Mathematically it can be shown that such a two-sided test is equivalent to a chi-square goodness of fit test involving one row of frequencies and two categories. Since the chi-square test involves an analysis of differences between obtained and expected frequencies regardless of the direction of the differences, there is no chi-square test procedure that is the equivalent of a one-sided test concerning the value of a population proportion.

Testing the Difference Between Two Population Proportions

A procedure for testing the null hypothesis that there is no difference between two proportions based on use of the normal probability distribution is presented in Chapter 11. Mathematically, it can be shown that such a two-tail test is equivalent to a chi-square contingency table test in which the observed frequencies are entered in a 2×2 table. Again, there is no chi-square test equivalent to a one-sided test based on use of the normal probability distribution.

The sampling procedure used in conjunction with testing the difference between two proportions is that *two* random samples are collected, one for each of two (k) categories. This contrasts with use of a 2×2 table for testing the independence of two variables, in which *one* random sample is collected for the overall analysis.

Testing the Difference Among Several Population Proportions

The chi-square test can be used to test the differences among several (k) population proportions by using a $2 \times k$ tabular design for the analysis of the frequencies. In this case, there is no mathematically equivalent procedure based on use of the z statistic. The null hypothesis is that the several population proportions are all mutually equal (or, that the several different sample proportions could have been obtained by chance from the same population). The sampling procedure is that several independent random samples are collected, one for each of the k data categories.

Solved Problems

Solved Problem 12.1 It is claimed that an equal number of men and women patronize a retail outlet specializing in the sale of jeans. A random sample of 40 customers is observed, with 25 being men and 15 being women. Test the null hypothesis that the overall number of men and women customers is equal by applying the chi-square test and using the 5 percent level of significance.

Solution:

H_0: The number of men and women customers is equal.
H_1: The number of men and women customers is not equal.

$$df = k - m - 1 = 2 - 0 - 1 = 1$$
$$\text{Critical } \chi^2 = 3.84 \text{ and calculated } \chi^2 = 2.50$$

The calculated test statistic of 2.50 is *not* greater than the critical value of 3.84. Therefore the null hypothesis cannot be rejected.

Solved Problem 12.2 With reference to Solved Problem 12.1, suppose it had instead been claimed that twice as many men as compared with women were store customers.

Solution:

H_0: There are twice as many men as there are women customers.
H_1: There are not twice as many men as women customers.

$$df = k - m - 1 = 2 - 0 - 1 = 1$$
$$\text{Critical } \chi^2 = 3.84 \text{ and calculated } \chi^2 = 0.31$$

The calculated chi-square statistic of 0.31 clearly does not exceed the critical value of 3.84. Therefore the null hypothesis cannot be rejected. The fact that neither of the null hypotheses in these two problems could be rejected demonstrates the benefit of the doubt given to the null hypothesis in each case.

Solved Problem 12.3 For the situation described in Solved Problem 12.1, suppose the same null hypothesis is tested, but that the sample frequencies in each category are exactly doubled. That is, of 80 randomly selected customers 50 are men and 30 are women. Test the null hypothesis at the 5 percent level of significance and compare your decision with the one in Solved Problem 12.1.

Solution:
H_0: The number of men and women customers is equal.
H_1: The number of men and women customers is not equal.

$$df = k - m - 1 = 2 - 0 - 1 = 1$$
$$\text{Critical } \chi^2 = 3.84 \text{ and calculated } \chi^2 = 5.00$$

The calculated chi-square value of 5.00 is greater than the critical value of 3.84. Therefore the null hypothesis is rejected at the 5 percent level of significance. Even though the sample data are proportionally the same as in Solved Problem 12.1, the decision now is to reject H_0 instead of accept H_0. This demonstrates the greater sensitivity of a statistical test associated with a larger sample size.

Chapter 13
ANALYSIS OF VARIANCE

IN THIS CHAPTER:

- ✔ Basic Rationale Associated with Testing the Differences among Several Population Means
- ✔ One-Factor Completely Randomized Design (One-Way ANOVA)
- ✔ Two-Way Analysis of Variance (Two-Way ANOVA)
- ✔ The Randomized Block Design (Two-Way ANOVA, One Observation per Cell)
- ✔ Two-Factor Completely Randomized Design (Two-Way ANOVA, n Observations per Cell)
- ✔ Solved Problem

Basic Rationale Associated with Testing the Differences among Several Population Means

Whereas the chi-square test can be used to test the differences among several population proportions, the analysis of variance can be used to test the differences among several population means. The null hypothesis is that the several population means are mutually equal. The sampling procedure used is to collect several independent random samples, one for each of the data categories (treatment levels).

The assumption underlying the use of the analysis of variance is that the several sample means were obtained from normally distributed populations having the same variance σ^2. However, the test procedure has been found to be relatively unaffected by violations of the normality assumption when the populations are unimodal and the sample sizes are approximately equal. Because the null hypothesis is that the population means are equal, the assumption of equal variance (*homogeneity of variance*) also implies that for practical purposes the test is concerned with the hypothesis that the means came from the same population. This is so because any normally distributed population is defined by the means the variance (or standard deviation) as the two parameters. All of the computational procedures presented in this chapter are for fixed-effects models as contrasted to random-effects models.

The basic rationale underlying the analysis of variance was first developed by the British statistician Ronald A. Fisher, and the F distribution was named in his honor. The conceptual rationale is as follows:

1. Compute the mean for each sample group and then determine the standard error of the means $s_{\bar{x}}$ *based only on the several sample means*. Computationally, this is the standard deviation of these several mean values.

2. Now, given the formula $s_{\bar{x}} = s / \sqrt{n}$ it follows that $s = \sqrt{n} s_{\bar{x}}$ and that $s^2 = n s_{\bar{x}}^2$. Therefore, the standard error of the mean computed in Step 1 above can be used to estimate the variance of the (common) population from which the several samples were obtained. This estimate of the population variance is called the *mean square among treatment groups*

(MSTR). Fisher called any variance estimate a mean square because computationally a variance is the mean of the squared deviations from the group mean.

3. Compute the variance separately for each sample group and with respect to each group mean. Then pool these variance values by weighting them according to $n - 1$ for each sample. This weighting procedure for the variance is an extension of the procedure for combining and weighting two sample variances. The resulting estimate of the population variance is called the *mean square error (MSE)* and is based on *within* group differences only. Again, it is called a mean square because it is a variance estimate. It is due to "error" because the deviations within each of the sample groups can be due only to random sampling error, and they cannot be due to any differences among the means of the population groups.

4. If the null hypothesis that $\mu_1 = \mu_2 \cdots = \mu_k$ is true, then it follows that each of the two mean squares obtained in Steps 2 and 3 above is an unbiased and independent estimator of the same population variance σ^2. However, if the null hypothesis is false, then the expected value of *MSTR* is larger than *MSE*. Essentially, any differences among the population means will inflate *MSTR* while having no effect on *MSE,* which is based on *within* group differences only.

5. Based on the observation in Step 4, the F distribution can be used to test the difference between the two variances. A one-sided test is involved, and the general form of the F test in the analysis of variance is:

$$F_{df_1, df_2} = MSTR \, / \, MSE$$

If the F ration is in the region of rejection for the specified level of significance, then the null hypothesis that the several population means are mutually equal is rejected.

Although the above steps are useful for describing the conceptual approach underlying the analysis of variance (ANOVA), the extension of this procedure for designs that are more complex than the simple comparison of k sample means is cumbersome. Therefore, in the following sections of this chapter each design is described in terms of the linear model that identifies the components influencing the random variable. Also, a standard analysis of variance table that includes the formulas that are needed for the calculation of the required mean square values is presented for each type of experimental design.

One-Factor Completely Randomized Design (One-Way ANOVA)

The one-way analysis of variance procedure is concerned with testing the difference among k sample means when the subjects are assigned randomly to each of the several treatment groups.

The linear equation, or model, that represents the one-factor completely randomized design is:

$$X_{ik} = \mu + \alpha_k + \varepsilon_{ik}$$

where μ = the overall mean of all k populations, α_k = effect of the treatment in the particular group k from which the value was sampled, and ε_{ik} = the random error associated with the process of sampling (ε is the Greek epsilon).

Table 13.1 is the summary table for the one-factor completely randomized design of the analysis of variance, including all computational formulas. The symbol system used in this table is somewhat different from that used in the previous section because of the need to use a system which can be extended logically to two-way analysis of variance. Thus, *MSTR* becomes the *mean square among the A treatment groups (MSA)*. Further, note that the definition of symbols in the context of analysis of variance is not necessarily consistent with the use of these symbols in general statistical analysis. For example, α_k is concerned with the effect on a randomly sampled value originating from the treatment group in which the value is located; it has nothing to do with the concept of α in general hypothesis testing procedures. Similarly, N in Table 13.1 designates the total size of the sample for all treatment groups combined, rather than a population size. New symbols included in Table 13.1 are T_k, which represents the sum (total) of the values in a particular treatment group, and T, which represents the sum of the sampled values in all groups combined.

Instead of the form of the null hypothesis described earlier, the general form of the null hypothesis in the analysis of variance makes reference to the relevant component of the linear model. Thus, for the one-way analysis of variance the null and alternative hypotheses can be stated as:

$$H_0: \mu_1 = \mu_2 = \cdots = \mu_k \quad \text{or equivalently,} \quad H_0: \alpha_k = 0$$

Source of variation	Degrees of freedom (df)	Sum of squares (SS)	Mean square (MS)	F ratio
Among treatment groups (A)	$K - 1$	$SSA = \sum_{k=1}^{K} \dfrac{T_k^2}{n_k} - \dfrac{T^2}{N}$	$MSA = \dfrac{SSA}{K - 1}$	$F = \dfrac{MSA}{MSE}$
Sampling error (E)	$N - K$	$SSE = SST - SSA$	$MSE = \dfrac{SSE}{N - K}$	
Total (T)	$N - 1$	$SST = \sum_{i=1}^{n} \sum_{k=1}^{K} X^2 - \dfrac{T^2}{N}$		

Table 13.1 Summary table for one-way analysis of variance (treatment groups need not be equal)

$$H_1: \text{not all } \mu_1 = \mu_2 = \cdots = \mu_k \qquad H_1: \alpha_k \neq 0.$$

Two-Way Analysis of Variance (Two-Way ANOVA)

Two-way analysis of variance is based on two dimensions of classifications, or treatments. For example, in analyzing the level of achievement in a training program we could consider both the effect of the method of instruction and the effect of prior school achievement. Similarly, we could investigate gasoline mileage according to the weight category of the car and according to the grade of gasoline. In data tables, the treatments identified in the column headings are typically called the *A* treatments; those in the row headings are called the *B* treatments.

Interaction in a two-factor experiment means that the two treatments are not independent, and that the effect to a particular treatment in one factor differs according to levels of the other factor.

 **Note!**

For example, in studying automobile mileage a higher-octane gasoline may improve mileage for certain types of cars but not for others.

In order to test for interaction, more than one observation or sampled measurement (i.e., *replication*) has to be included in each cell of the two-way data table.

The Randomized Block Design (Two-Way ANOVA, One Observation per Cell)

The two-way analysis of variance model in which there is only one observation per cell is generally referred to as the *randomized block design*, because of the principal use for this model. What if we extend the idea of using paired observations to compare two sample means to the basic one-way analysis of variance model and have groups of *k matched* individuals assigned randomly to each treatment level? In analysis of variance, such matched groups are called *blocks*, and because the individuals (or items) are randomly assigned based on the identified block membership, the design is referred to as the randomized block design.

In such a design the blocks dimension is not a treatment dimension as such. The objective of using this design is not for the specific purpose of testing for a blocks effect. Rather, by being able to assign some of the variability among subjects to prior achievement, for example, the *MSE* can be reduced and the resulting test of the *A* treatments effects is more sensitive.

The linear model for the two-way analysis of variance model with one observation per cell (with no replication) is:

$$X_{jk} = \mu + \beta_j + \alpha_k + \varepsilon_{jk}$$

where μ = the overall mean regardless of any treatment, β_j = effect of the treatment *j* or block *j* in the *B* dimension of classification, α_k = effect of the treatment *k* in the *A* dimension of classification, and ε_{jk} = the random error associated with the process sampling.

Table 13.2 is the summary table for the two-way analysis of variance without replication. As compared with Table 13.1 for the one-way analysis of variance, the only new symbol in this table is T_j^2, which indicates that the total of each *j* group (for the *B* treatments, or blocks) is squared.

Two-Factor Completely Randomized Design (Two-Way ANOVA, *n* Observations Per Cell)

When replication is included within a two-way design, the interaction between the two factors can be tested. Thus, when such a design is used, three different null hypotheses can be tested by the analysis of variance: that there are no column effects (the column means are not significantly different), that there are no row effects (the row means are not significantly different), and that there is no interaction between the two facts (the two factors are independent).

A significant interaction effect indicates that the effect of treatments

Source of variation	Degrees of freedom (df)	Sum of Squares (SS)	Mean square (MS)	F ratio
Among treatment groups (A)	$K - 1$	$SSA = \sum_{k=1}^{K} \dfrac{T_k^2}{n_k} - \dfrac{T^2}{N}$	$MSA = \dfrac{SSA}{K - 1}$	$F = \dfrac{MSA}{MSE}$
Among treatment groups, or blocks (B)	$J - 1$	$SSB = \dfrac{1}{K}\sum_{j=1}^{J} T_j^2 - \dfrac{T^2}{N}$	$MSB = \dfrac{SSB}{J - 1}$	$F = \dfrac{MSB}{MSE}$
Sampling error (E)	$(J - 1)(K - 1)$	$SSE = SST - SSA - SSB$	$MSE = \dfrac{SSE}{(J - 1)(K - 1)}$	
Total (T)	$N - 1$	$SST = \sum_{j=1}^{J}\sum_{k=1}^{K} X^2 - \dfrac{T^2}{N}$		

Table 13.2 Summary table for two-way analysis of variance with one observation per cell (randomized block design)

for one factor varies according to levels of the other factor. In such a case, the existence of column and/or row effects may not be meaningful from the standpoint of the application of research results.

The linear model for the two-way analysis of variance when replication is included is:

$$X_{ijk} = \mu + \beta_j + \alpha_k + \iota_{jk} + \varepsilon_{ijk}$$

where μ = the overall mean regardless of any treatment, β_j = effect of the treatment j in the B (row) dimension, α_k = effect of the treatment k in the A (column) dimension, ι_{jk} = interaction between treatment j (of factor B) and treatment k (of factor A) (where ι is the Greek iota), and ε_{ijk} = the random error associated with the process of sampling.

Table 13.3 is the summary table for the two-way analysis of variance with replication. The formulas included in this table are based on the assumption that there are an equal number of observations in all of the cells.

Solved Problem

Solved Problem 13.1 Fifteen trainees in a technical program are randomly assigned to three different types of instructional approaches, all of which are concerned with developing a specified level of skill in computer-assisted design. The achievement test scores at the conclusion of the instructional unit are reported in Table 13.4, along with the mean performance score associated with each instructional approach. Use the analysis of variance procedure to test the null hypothesis that the three sample means were obtained from the sample population, using the 5 percent level of significance for the test.

Solution:

1. The overall mean of all 15 test scores is 80. The standard error of the mean, based on the three sample means as reported, is 5.0.
2. MSTR = 125.0.
3. MSE = 37.3.
4. Since MSTR is larger than MSE, a test of the null hypothesis is appropriate.

Source of variation	Degrees of freedom (df)	Sum of Squares (SS)	Mean square (MS)	F ratio
Among treatment groups (A)	$K - 1$	$SSA = \sum_{k=1}^{K} \dfrac{T_k^2}{nJ} - \dfrac{T^2}{N}$	$MSA = \dfrac{SSA}{K - 1}$	$F = \dfrac{MSA}{MSE}$
Among treatment groups (B)	$J - 1$	$SSB = \sum_{j=1}^{J} \dfrac{T_j^2}{nK} - \dfrac{T^2}{N}$	$MSB = \dfrac{SSB}{J - 1}$	$F = \dfrac{MSB}{MSE}$
Interaction (between) factors (A and B) (I)	$(J - 1)(K - 1)$	$SSI = \dfrac{1}{n} \sum_{j=1}^{J} \sum_{k=1}^{K} \left(\sum_{i=1}^{n} X \right)^2 - SSA - SSB - \dfrac{T^2}{N}$	$MSI = \dfrac{SSI}{(J - 1)(K - 1)}$	$F = \dfrac{MSI}{MSE}$
Sampling error (E)	$JK(n - 1)$	$SSE = SST - SSA - SSB - SSI$	$MSE = \dfrac{SSE}{JK(n - 1)}$	
Total (T)	$N - 1$	$SST = \sum_{i=1}^{n} \sum_{j=1}^{J} \sum_{k=1}^{K} X^2 - \dfrac{T^2}{N}$		

Table 13.3 Summary table for two-way analysis of variance with more than one observation per cell

Instructional method	Test scores					Total scores	Mean test scores
A_1	86	79	81	70	84	400	80
A_2	90	76	88	82	89	425	85
A_3	82	68	73	71	81	375	75

Table 13.4 Achievement test scores of trainees under three methods of instruction

Critical F $(2, 12; \alpha = 0.05) = 3.88$.

5. $F = MSTR/MSE = 3.35$

Because the calculated F statistic of 3.35 is not greater than the critical F value of 3.88, the null hypothesis that the mean test scores for the three instructional methods in the population are all mutually equal cannot be rejected at the 5 percent level of significance.

Chapter 14

LINEAR REGRESSION AND CORRELATION ANALYSIS

IN THIS CHAPTER:

- ✔ *Objectives and Assumptions of Regression Analysis*
- ✔ *The Method of Least Squares for Fitting a Regression Line*
- ✔ *Residuals and Residual Plots*
- ✔ *The Standard Error of Estimate*
- ✔ *Inferences Concerning the Slope*
- ✔ *Confidence Intervals for the Conditional Mean*
- ✔ *Prediction Intervals for Individual Values of the Dependent Variable*
- ✔ *The Coefficient of Determination*

✔ *The Coefficient of Correlation*
✔ *Solved Problems*

Objectives and Assumptions of Regression Analysis

The primary objective of regression analysis is to estimate the value of a random variable (the *dependent variable*) given that the value of an associated variable (the *independent variable*) is known. The dependent variable is also called the *response variable*, while the independent variable is also called the *predictor variable*. The *regression equation* is the algebraic formula by which the estimated value of the dependent, or response, variable is determined.

The term *simple regression analysis* indicates that the value of a dependent variable is estimated on the basis of one independent, or predictor, variable. *Multiple regression analysis* is concerned with estimating the value of a dependent variable on the basis of two or more independent variables.

The Method of Least Squares for Fitting a Regression Line

The linear equation that represents the simple linear regression model is:

$$Y_i = \beta_0 + \beta_1 X_i + \varepsilon_i$$

where Y_i = value of the dependent variable in the *i*th trial, or observation; β_0 = first parameter of the regression equation, which indicates the value of Y when $X = 0$; β_1 = second parameter of the regression equation, which indicates the slope of the regression line; X_i = the specified value of the independent variable in the *i*th trial, or observation; and ε_i = random-sampling error in the *i*th trial, or observation (ε is the Greek epsilon)

The parameters β_0 and β_1 in the linear regression model are estimated by the values b_0 and b_1 that are based on sample data. Thus the linear regression equation based on sample data that is used to estimate a single (conditional) value of the dependent variable, where the "hat" over the Y indicates that it is an estimated value, is:

$$\hat{Y} = b_0 + b_1 X$$

Depending on the mathematical criterion used, a number of different linear equations can be developed for a given scatter plot. By the *least-squares criterion* the best-fitting regression line (and the best equation) is that for which the sum of the squared deviations between the estimated and actual values of the dependent variable for the sample data is minimized. The computational formulas by which the values of b_0 and b_1 in the regression equation can be determined for the equation which satisfies the least-squares criterion are:

$$b_1 = \frac{\Sigma XY - n\overline{X}\,\overline{Y}}{\Sigma X^2 - n\overline{X}^2}$$

$$b_0 = \overline{Y} - b_1\overline{X}$$

Once the regression equation is formulated, then this equation can be used to estimate the value of the dependent variable given the value of the independent variable. However, such estimation should be done only within the range of the values of the independent variable originally sampled, since there is no statistical basis to assume that the regression line is appropriate outside these limits. Further, it should be determined whether the relationship expressed by the regression equation is real or could have occurred in the sample data purely by chance.

Residuals and Residual Plots

For a given value X of the independent variable, the regression line value $\hat{Y}$ often is called the *fitted value* of the dependent variable. The difference between the observed value Y and the fitted value $\hat{Y}$ in called the *residual* for that observation and is denoted by e:

$$e = Y - \hat{Y}.$$

A *residual plot* is obtained by plotting the residuals e with respect to the independent variable X or, alternatively, with respect to the fitted regression line values $\hat{Y}$. Such a plot can be used as an alternative to the use of the scatter plot to investigate whether the assumptions concerning linearity and equality of conditional variances appear to be satisfied. Residual plots are particularly important in multiple regression analysis.

The set of residuals for the sample data also serve as the basis for calculating the standard error of estimate, as described in the following section.

The Standard Error of Estimate

The *standard error of estimate* is the conditional standard deviation of the dependent variable Y given a value of the independent variable X. For population data, the standard error of estimate is represented by the symbol $\sigma_{Y.X}$. The deviations formula by which this value is estimated on the basis of sample data is:

$$s_{Y.X} = \sqrt{\frac{\Sigma(Y - \hat{Y})^2}{n-2}} = \sqrt{\frac{\Sigma e^2}{n-2}}$$

Note that the numerator in the formula is the sum of the squares of the residuals described in the preceding section. Although the formula clearly reflects the idea that the standard error of estimate is the standard deviation with respect to the regression line (that is, it is the standard deviation of the vertical "scatter" about the line), computationally the formula requires that every fitted value $\hat{Y}$ be calculated for the sample data. The alternative computational formula, which does not require determination of each fitted value and is therefore generally easier to use is:

$$s_{Y.X} = \sqrt{\frac{\Sigma Y^2 - b_0 \Sigma Y - b_1 \Sigma XY}{n-2}}$$

As will be seen in the following sections, the standard error of estimate serves as the cornerstone for the various standard errors used in the hypothesis testing and interval-estimation procedures in regression analysis.

Inferences Concerning the Slope

Before a regression equation is used for the purpose of estimation or prediction, we should first determine if a relationship appears to exist between the two variables in the population, or whether the observed relationship in the sample could have occurred by chance. In the absence of any relationship in the population, the slope of the population regression line would, by definition, be zero: $\beta_1 = 0$. Therefore, the usual null hypothesis tested is $H_0 : \beta_1 = 0$. The null hypothesis can also be formulated as a one-tail test, in which case the alternative hypothesis is not simply that the two variables are related, but that the relationship is of a specific type (direct or inverse).

A hypothesized value of the slope is tested by computing a t statistic and using $n - 2$ degrees of freedom. Two degrees of freedom are lost in the process of interference because *two* parameters estimates, b_0 and b_1, are included in the regression equation. The standard formula is:

$$t = \frac{b_1 - (\beta_1)_0}{s_{b_1}}$$

where

$$s_{b_1} = \frac{s_{Y.X}}{\sqrt{\Sigma X^2 - n\overline{X}^2}}$$

However, when the null hypothesis is that the slope is zero, which generally is the hypothesis, then the first formula is simplified and is stated as:

$$t = \frac{b_1}{s_{b_1}}$$

The confidence interval for the population slope β_1, in which the degrees of freedom associated with the t are once again $n - 2$, is constructed as follows:

$$b_1 \pm t s_{b_1}$$

Confidence Intervals for the Conditional Mean

The point estimate for the conditional *mean* of the dependent variable, given a specific value of X, is the regression line value $\hat{Y}$. When we use the regression equation to estimate the conditional *mean*, the appropriate symbol for the conditional mean of Y that is estimated is $\hat{\mu}_Y$:

$$\hat{\mu}_Y = b_0 + b_1 X$$

Based on sample data, the standard error of the conditional mean varies in value according to the designated value of X and is:

$$s_{\bar{Y}.X} = s_{Y.X} \sqrt{\frac{1}{n} + \frac{(X - \bar{X})^2}{\Sigma X^2 - [(\Sigma X)^2 / n]}}$$

Given the point estimate of the conditional mean and the standard error of the conditional mean, the confidence interval for the conditional mean, using $n - 2$ degrees of freedom, is:

$$\hat{\mu}_Y \pm t s_{\bar{Y}.X}$$

Again, it is $n - 2$ degrees of freedom because the two parameter estimates b_0 and b_1 are required in the regression equation.

Prediction Intervals for Individual Values of the Dependent Variable

As contrasted to a confidence interval, which is concerned with estimating a population parameter, a *prediction interval* is concerned with estimating an *individual* value and is therefore a probability interval. It might seem that a prediction interval could be constructed by using only the standard error of estimate. However, such an interval would be incomplete, because the standard error of estimate does not include the uncertainty associated with the fact that the position of the regression line based on sample data includes sampling error and generally is not identical to the population regression line. The complete standard error for a prediction interval is called the *standard error of forecast*, and it includes the uncertainty associated with the position of the regression line value itself. The basic formula for the standard error of forecast is:

$$s_{Y(next)} = \sqrt{s_{Y.X}^2 + s_{\bar{Y}.X}^2}$$

The computational version of the formula for the standard error of forecast is:

$$s_{Y(next)} = s_{Y.X}\sqrt{1 + \frac{1}{n} + \frac{(X - \bar{X})^2}{\Sigma X^2 - [(\Sigma X)^2 / n]}}$$

Finally, the prediction interval for an individual value of the dependent variable, using $n - 2$ degrees of freedom, is:

$$\hat{Y} \pm ts_{Y(next)}$$

The Coefficient of Determination

Consider that if an individual value of the dependent variable Y were estimated without knowledge of the value of any other variable, then the variance associated with this estimate, and the basis for constructing a prediction interval, would be the variance σ_Y^2. Given a value of X, however, the variance associated with the estimate is reduced and is represented by $\sigma_{Y.X}^2$. If there is a relationship between the two variables, then $\sigma_{Y.X}^2$ will always be smaller than σ_Y^2. For a perfect relationship, in which all values of the dependent variable are equal to the respective fitted regression line values, $\sigma_{Y.X}^2 = 0$. Therefore, in the absence of a perfect relationship, the value of $\sigma_{Y.X}^2$ indicates the uncertainty remaining *after* consideration of the value of the independent variable. Or, we can say that the ratio of $\sigma_{Y.X}^2$ to σ_Y^2 indicates the proportion of variance (uncertainty) in the dependent variable that remains unexplained after a specific value of the independent variable has been given:

$$\frac{\sigma_{Y.X}^2}{\sigma_Y^2} = \frac{\text{unexplained variance remaining in } Y}{\text{total variance in } Y}$$

Given the proportion of unexplained variance, a useful measure of relationship is the *coefficient of determination* minus the complement of the above ratio, indicating the proportion of variance in the dependent variable that is statistically *explained* by the regression equation (i.e., by knowledge of the associated independent variable X). For population data the coefficient of determination is represented by the Greek ρ^2 (rho squared) and is determined by:

$$\rho^2 = 1 - \frac{\sigma_{Y.X}^2}{\sigma_Y^2}$$

proportion of explained variance = 1 − (proportion of unexplained variance)

For sample data, the estimated value of the coefficient of determination can be obtained by the corresponding formula:

$$r^2 = 1 - \frac{s_{Y.X}^2}{s_Y^2}$$

For computational purposes, the following formula for the sample coefficient of determination is convenient:

$$r^2 = \frac{b_0 \Sigma Y + b_1 \Sigma XY - n\overline{Y}^2}{\Sigma Y^2 - n\overline{Y}^2}$$

The Coefficient of Correlation

Although the coefficient of determination r^2 is relatively easy to interpret, it does not lend itself to statistical testing. However, the square root of the coefficient of determination, which is called the *coefficient of correlation r,* does lend itself to statistical testing because it can be used to define a test statistic that is distributed as the t distribution when the population correlation ρ equals 0. The value of the correlation coefficient can range from − 1.00 to +1.00. The arithmetic sign associated with the correlation coefficient, which is always the same as the sign associated with β_1 in the regression equation, indicates the direction of the relationship between X and Y (positive = direct; negative =

inverse). The coefficient of correlation for population data, with the arithmetic sign being the same as that for the slope β_1 in the regression equation, is:

$$\rho = \sqrt{\rho^2}$$

The coefficient of correlation for sample data, with the arithmetic sign being the same as that for the sample slope b_1, is:

$$r = \sqrt{r^2}$$

In summary, the sign of the correlation coefficient indicates the direction of the relationship between the X and Y variables, while the absolute value of the coefficient indicates the extent of relationship. The squared value of the correlation coefficient is the coefficient of determination and indicates the proportion of the variance in Y explained by knowledge of X (and vice versa).

The following formula does not require prior determination of the regression values of b_0 and b_1. This formula would be used when the purpose of the analysis is to determine the extent and type of relationship between two variables, but without an accompanying interest in estimating Y given X. When this formula is used, the sign of the correlation coefficient is determined automatically, without the necessity of observing or calculating the slope of the regression line. The formula is:

$$r = \frac{n \sum XY - \sum X \sum Y}{\sqrt{n \sum X^2 - (\sum X)^2} \sqrt{n \sum Y^2 - (\sum Y)^2}}$$

Solved Problems

Solved Problem 14.1 Suppose an analyst takes a random sample of 10 recent truck shipments made by a company and records the distance in miles and delivery time to the nearest half-day from the time that the shipment was made available for pickup. Construct the scatter plot for the data in Table 14.1 and consider whether the linear regression analysis appears appropriate.

Sampled shipment	1	2	3	4	5	6	7	8	9	10
Distance (X), miles	825	215	1,070	550	480	920	1,350	325	670	1,215
Delivery time (Y), days	3.5	1.0	4.0	2.0	1.0	3.0	4.5	1.5	3.0	5.0

Table 14.1 Sample observations of trucking distance and delivery time for 10 randomly selected shipments

Solution: The scatter plot for these data is portrayed in Figure 14-1. The first reported pair of values in the table is represented by the dot entered above 825 on the X axis and aligned with 3.5 with respect to the Y axis. The other nine points in the scatter plot were similarly entered. From the diagram, it appears that the plotted points generally follow a linear relationship and the vertical scatter at the line is about the same for the low values and high values of X. Thus linear regression analysis appears appropriate.

Solved Problem 14.2 Determine the least-squares regression equation for the data in Solved Problem 14.1, and enter the regression line on the scatter plot for these data.

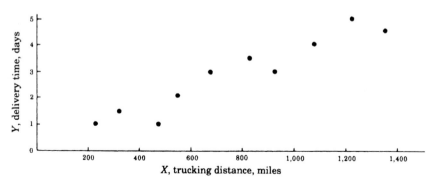

Figure 14-1

Solution:

$$b_1 = \frac{\sum XY - n\overline{X}\,\overline{Y}}{\sum X^2 - n\overline{X}^2} = 0.0035851 \cong 0.0036$$

$$b_0 = \overline{Y} - b\overline{X} = 0.1068 \cong 0.11$$

$$\hat{Y} = b_0 + b_1 X = 0.11 + 0.0036X$$

Solved Problem 14.3 Using the regression equation developed in Solved Problem 14.2, estimate the delivery time from the time that the shipment is available for pickup for a shipment of 1,000 miles. Could this regression equation be used to estimate delivery time for a shipment of 2,500 miles?

Solution:

$$\hat{Y} = 0.11 + 0.0036X = 3.71 \, days$$

It is not appropriate to use the above equation for a trip of 2,500 miles because the sample data for this estimated linear regression equation included trips up to 1,350 miles distance only.

Chapter 15
MULTIPLE REGRESSION AND CORRELATION

IN THIS CHAPTER:

✔ *Objectives and Assumptions of Multiple Regression Analysis*
✔ *Additional Concepts in Multiple Regression Analysis*
✔ *The Use of Indicator (Dummy) Variables*
✔ *Analysis of Variance in Linear Regression Analysis*
✔ *Objectives and Assumptions of Multiple Correlation Analysis*
✔ *Solved Problem*

Objectives and Assumptions of Multiple Regression Analysis

Multiple regression analysis is an extension of simple regression analysis to applications involving the use of two or more independent variables (predictors) to estimate the value of the dependent variable (response variable). In the case of two independent variables, denoted by X_1 and X_2, the linear algebraic model is:

$$Y_i = \beta_0 + \beta_1 X_{i,1} + \beta_2 X_{i,2} + \varepsilon_i$$

The definitions of the above terms are equivalent to the definitions for simple regression analysis, except that more than one independent variable is involved in the present case. Based on the sample data, the linear regression equation for the case of two independent variables is:

$$\hat{Y} = b_0 + b_1 X_1 + b_2 X_2$$

The multiple regression equation identifies the best-fitting line based on the method of least squares. In the case of multiple regression analysis, the best-fitting line is a line through n-dimensional space. The assumptions of multiple linear regression analysis are similar to those of the simple case involving only one independent variable. For point estimation, the principal assumptions are:

1. The dependent variable is a random variable.
2. The relationship between the several independent variables and the one dependent variable is linear.
3. The variances of the conditional distributions of the dependent variable, given various combinations of values of the independent variables, are all equal.
4. The conditional distributions of the dependent variable are normally distributed.
5. The observed values of the dependent variable are independent of each other.

Violation of assumption 5 is called *autocorrelation*.

Additional Concepts in Multiple Regression Analysis

Constant
Although the b_0 and the several b_i values are all estimates of parameters in the regression equation, in most computer output the term *con-*

stant refers to the value of the b_0 intercept. In multiple regression analysis, this is the regression equation value of the dependent variable Y given that all of the independent variables are equal to zero.

Partial regression coefficient

Each of the b_1 regression coefficients is in fact a partial regression coefficient. A partial regression coefficient is the conditional coefficient given that one or more other independent variables (and their coefficients) are also included in the regression equation. Conceptually, a partial regression coef-ficient represents the slope of the regression line between the independent variable of interest and the dependent variable given that the other independent variables are included in the model and are thereby statistically "held constant." The symbol $b_{Y1.2}$ is the partial regression coefficient for the first independent variable given that a second independent variable is also included in the regression equation. For simplicity, when the entire regression equation is presented, this coefficient usually is designated by b_1.

Use of the *F* Test

The analysis of variance is used in regression analysis to test for the significance of the overall model, as contrasted to considering the significance of the individual independent variables by use of *t* tests, below.

Use of the *t* Tests

The *t* tests are used to determine if the partial regression coefficient for each independent variable represents a significant contribution to the overall model.

Confidence interval for the conditional mean

Where the standard error of the conditional mean in the case of two independent variables is designated by $s_{\bar{Y}.12}$, the formula for the confidence interval is:

$$\hat{\mu}_Y \pm t s_{\bar{Y}.12}$$

Prediction intervals

The prediction interval for estimating the value of an individual observation of the dependent variable, given the values of the several independent variables, is similar to the prediction interval in simple regression analysis. The general formula for the prediction interval is:

$$\hat{Y} \pm ts_{Y(next)}$$

Stepwise regression analysis

In forward stepwise regression analysis, one independent variable is added to the model in each step of selecting such variables for inclusion in the final model. In backward stepwise regression analysis, we begin with all the variables under consideration being included in the model, and then (possibly) we remove one variable in each step. These are two of several available approaches to choosing the "best" set of independent variables for the model.

The Use of Indicator (Dummy) Variables

Although the linear regression model is based upon the independent variables being on a quantitative measurement scale, it is possible to include a qualitative variable in a multiple regression model. Examples of such variables are the sex of an employee in a study of salary levels and the location codes in a real estate appraisal model.

The indicator variable utilizes a binary 0,1 code. Where k designates the number of categories that exist for the qualitative variable, $k - 1$ indicator variables are required to code the qualitative variable. Thus, the sex of an employee can be coded by one indicator variable, because $k = 2$ in this case. The code system then can be $0 =$ female and $1 =$ male. For a real estate appraisal model in which there are three types of locations, labeled A, B, C, $k = 3$ and therefore $3 - 1 = 2$ indicator variables are required. The difficulty associated with having a qualitative variable that has more than two categories is that more than one indicator is required to represent the variable in the regression equation.

Analysis of Variance in Linear Regression Analysis

An F test is used to test for the significance of the overall model. That is, it is used to test the null hypothesis that there is no relationship in the population between the independent variables taken as a group and the one dependent variable. Specifically, the null hypothesis states that *all* of the net regression coefficients in the regression equation for the population are equal to zero. Therefore, for the case of two independent variables, or predictors, the null hypothesis with respect to the F test is $H_0 : \beta_1 = \beta_2 = 0$.

If there is only one independent variable in the regression model, then the F test is equivalent to a two-tail t test directed at the slope b_1. Therefore use of the F test is not required in simple regression analysis. For clarity, however, we focus on the simple regression model to explain the rationale of using the analysis of variance.

Consider the scatter plot in Figure 15-1. If there is no regression effect in the population, then the $\hat{Y}$ line differs from the $\bar{Y}$ line purely y chance. It follows that the variance estimate based on the differences, called *mean square regression (MSR)*, would be different only by chance from the variance estimated based on the residuals, called *mean square error (MSE)*. On the other hand, if there is a regression effect, then the mean square regression is inflated in value as compared with the mean square error. Table 15.1 presents the standard format for the analysis of variance table that is used to test for the significance of an overall regression effect. The degrees of freedom k associated with MSR in the table are the number of independent variables in the multiple regression equation. As indicated in the table, the test statistic is:

$$F = MSR/MSE$$

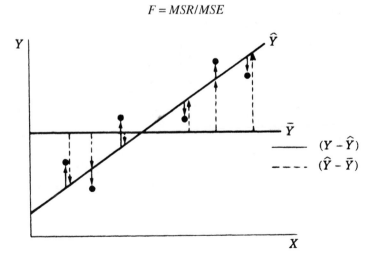

Figure 15-1

Source of variation	Degrees of freedom (df)	Sum of squares (SS)	Mean square (MS)	F ratio
Regression (R)	k	SSR	$MSR = \dfrac{SSR}{k}$	$F = \dfrac{MSR}{MSE}$
Sampling error (E)	$n - k - 1$	SSE	$MSE = \dfrac{SSE}{n - k - 1}$	
Total (T)	$n - 1$	SST		

Table 15.1 Analysis of variance table for testing the significance of the regression effect

Objectives and Assumptions of Multiple Correlation Analysis

Multiple correlation analysis is an extension of simple correlation analysis to situations involving two or more independent variables and their degree of association with the dependent variable. As is the case for multiple regression analysis, the dependent variable is designated Y while the several independent variables are designated sequentially beginning with X_1.

The *coefficient of multiple correlation,* which is designated by the uppercase $R_{Y.12}$ for the case of two independent variables, is indicative of the extent of relationship between two independent variables taken as a group and the dependent variable. It is possible that one of the independent variables alone could have a positive relationship with the dependent variable while the other independent variable could have a negative relationship with the dependent variable.

Remember

All *R* values are reported as absolute values.

The *coefficient of multiple determination* is designated by $R_{Y.12}^2$ for the case of two independent variables. Similar to the interpretation of the simple coefficient of determination, this coefficient indicates the proportion of variance in the dependent variable that is statistically accounted for by knowledge of the two (or more) independent variables. The sample coefficient of multiple determination for the case of two independent variables is:

$$R_{Y.12}^2 = 1 - \frac{s_{Y.12}^2}{s_Y^2}$$

The assumptions of multiple correlation analysis are similar to those of the simple case involving only one independent variable. These are:

1. All variables involved in the analysis are random variables.
2. The relationships are all linear.
3. The conditional variances are all equal.
4. For each variable, observed values are independent of other observed values for that variable.
5. The conditional distributions are all normal.

These requirements are quite stringent and are seldom completely satisfied in real data situations.

Solved Problem

Solved Problem 15.1 Refer to the residual plot in Figure 15-2, which plots the residuals with respect to the fitted values, and observe whether the requirements of linearity and equality of conditional variances appear to be satisfied.

Solution: The assumption of linearity appears to be satisfied. With respect to the equality of the conditional variances, however, it appears that the conditional variances may be somewhat greater at large values of the estimated salary, beyond $60,000 on the horizontal scale of the residual plot.

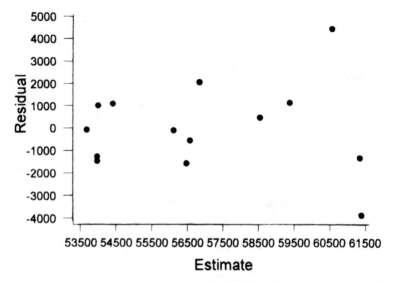

Figure 15-2 Residual plot for the fitted values.

Chapter 16

TIME SERIES ANALYSIS AND BUSINESS FORECASTING

IN THIS CHAPTER:

143

✔ *Exponential Smoothing as a Forecasting Method*

✔ *Other Forecasting Methods That Incorporate Smoothing*

✔ *Solved Problems*

The Classical Time Series Model

A *time series* is a set of observed values, such as production or sales data, for a sequentially ordered series of time periods. A time series is portrayed graphically by a line graph, with the time periods represented on the horizontal axis and time series values represented on the vertical axis.

Time series analysis is the procedure by which the time-related factors that influence the values observed in the time series are identified and segregated. Once identified, they can be used to aid in the interpretation of historical time series values and to forecast future time series values. The classical approach to time series analysis identifies four such influences, or *components*:

1. *Trend* (T): The general long-term movement in the time series values over an extended period of years.

2. *Cyclical fluctuations* (C): Recurring up and down movements with respect to trend that have a duration of several years.

3. *Seasonal variations* (S): Up and down movements with respect to trend that are completed within a year and recur annually.

4. *Irregular variations* (I): The erratic variations from trend that cannot be ascribed to the cyclical or seasonal influences.

The model underlying classical time series analysis is based on the assumption that for any designated period in the time series the value of the variable is determined by the four components defined above, and, furthermore, that the components have a multiplicative relationship. Thus, where Y represents the observed time series value,

$$Y = T \times C \times S \times I$$

The model represented is used as the basis for separating the influences of the various components that affect time series values.

Trend Analysis

Because trend analysis is concerned with the long-term direction of movement in the time series, such analysis generally is performed using annual data. Typically, at least 15 or 20 years of data should be used, so that cyclical movements involving several years duration are not taken to be indicative of the overall trend of the time series values.

The method of least squares is the most frequent basis used for identifying the trend component of the time series by determining the equation for the best-fitting trend line. Note that statistically speaking, a trend line is not a regression line, since the dependent variable Y is not a random variable, but, rather, a series of historical values. Further, there can be only one historical value for any given time period and the values associated with adjoining time periods are likely to be dependent, rather than independent. Nevertheless, the least-squares method is a convenient basis for determining the trend component of a time series. When the long-term increase or decrease appears to follow a linear trend, the equation for the trend-line values, with X representing the year, is $Y_T = b_0 + b_1 X$. The b_0 represents the point of intersection of the trend line with the Y axis, whereas the b_1 represents the slope of the trend line. Where X is the year and Y is the observed time-series value, the formulas for determining the values of b_0 and b_1 for the linear trend equation are:

$$b_1 = \frac{\Sigma XY - n\overline{X}\,\overline{Y}}{\Sigma X^2 - n\overline{X}^2} \qquad b_0 = \overline{Y} - b_1\overline{X}$$

In the case of nonlinear trend, two types of trend curves often found to be useful are the exponential trend curve and the parabolic trend curve. A typical *exponential trend curve* is one that reflects a constant rate of growth during a period of years. An exponential curve is so named because the independent variable X is the exponent of b_1 in the general equation: $Y_T = b_0 b_1^X$, where b_0 = value of Y_T in Year 0 and b_1 = rate of growth. Taking the logarithm of both sides of the above formula results in linear logarithmic trend equation,

$$\log Y_T = \log b_0 + X \log b_1$$

The advantage of the transformation into logarithms is that the linear equation for trend analysis can be applied to the logs of the values when the time series follows an exponential curve. The forecasted log values for Y_T can then be reconverted to the original measurement units by taking the antilog of the values.

Important ✔

Many time series for the sales of a particular product can be observed to include three stages: an *introductory stage* of slow growth in sales; a *middle stage* of rapid sales increases; and a *final stage* of slow growth as market saturation is reached.

Analysis of Cyclical Variations

Annual time series values represent the effects of only the trend and cyclical components, because the seasonal and irregular components are defined as short-run influences. Therefore, for annual data the cyclical component can be identified as being the component that would remain in the data after the influence of the trend component is removed. This removal is accomplished by dividing each of the observed values by the associated trend value, as follows:

$$\frac{Y}{Y_T} = \frac{T \times C}{T} = C$$

The ratio is multiplied by 100 so that the mean cyclical relative will be 100. A cyclical relative of 100 would indicate the absence of any cyclical influence on the annual time series value. In order to aid in the interpretation of cyclical relatives, a cycle chart that portrays the cyclical relatives according to year is often prepared.

Measurement of Seasonal Variations

The influence of the seasonal component on time series values is identified by determining the seasonal index associated with each month (or quarter) of the year. The arithmetic mean of all 12 monthly index numbers is 100. The identification of positive and negative seasonal influences is important for production and inventory planning.

The procedure most frequently used to determine seasonal index numbers is the *ratio-to-moving-average method*. By this method, the ratio of each monthly value to the moving average centered at that month is first determined. Because a moving average based on monthly data  for an entire year would average out the seasonal and irregular fluctuations, but not the longer-term trend and cyclical influences, the ratio of a monthly value to a moving average can be represented symbolically by:

$$\frac{Y}{Moving\ average} = \frac{T \times C \times S \times I}{T \times C} = S \times I$$

The second step in the ratio-to-moving-average method is to average out the irregular component. This is typically done by listing the several ratios applicable to the same month for the several years, eliminating the highest and lowest values, and computing the mean of the remaining ratios. The resulting mean is called a *modified mean*, because of the elimination of the two extreme values. The final step in the ratio-to-moving-average method is to adjust the modified mean ratios by a correction factor so that the sum of the 12 monthly ratios is 1,200.

Applying Seasonal Adjustments

One frequent application of seasonal indexes is that of adjusting observed time series data by removing the influence of the seasonal component from the data. Such adjusted data are called *seasonally adjusted data*, or *deseasonalized data*.

Note!

Seasonal adjustments are particularly relevant if we wish to compare data for different months to determine if an increase or decrease relative to seasonal expectations has taken place.

The observed monthly time series values are adjusted for seasonal influence by dividing each value by the monthly index for that month. The result is then multiplied by 100 to maintain the decimal position of the original data. The process of adjusting data for the influence of seasonal variations can be represented by:

$$\frac{Y}{S} = \frac{T \times C \times S \times I}{S} = T \times C \times I$$

Although the resulting values after the application are in the same measurement units as the original data, they do not represent actual data. Rather, they are relative values and are meaningful for comparative purposes only.

Forecasting Based on Trend and Seasonal Factors

A beginning point for long-term forecasting of annual values is provided by use of the trend-line equation. However, a particularly important consideration in long-term forecasting is the cyclical component of the time series. There is no standard method by which the cyclical component can be forecast based on historical time series values alone, but certain economic indicators are useful for anticipating cyclical turning points.

For short-term forecasting one possible approach is to deseasonalize the most-recent observed value and then to multiply this deseasonalized value by the seasonal index for the forecast period. This approach assumes that the only difference between the two periods will be the difference that is attributable to the seasonal influence. An alternative approach is to use the projected trend value as the basis for the forecast and then adjust it for the seasonal component. When the equation for the trend line is based on annual values, one must first "step down" the equation so that it is expressed in terms of months. A trend equation based on annual data is modified to obtain projected monthly values as follows:

$$Y_T = \frac{b_0}{12} + \frac{b_1}{144} X$$

A trend equation based on annual data is modified to obtain projected quarterly values as follows:

$$Y_T = \frac{b_0}{4} + \frac{b_1}{16} X$$

The basis for the above modifications is not obvious if one overlooks the fact that trend values are not associated with points in time, but rather, with periods of time. Because of this consideration, all three elements in the equation for annual trend have to be stepped down.

Cyclical Forecasting and Business Indicators

Forecasting based on the trend and seasonal components of a time series is considered only a beginning point in economic forecasting. One reason is the necessity to consider the likely effect of the cyclical component during the forecast period, while the second is the importance of identifying the specific causative factors which have influenced the time series variables.

For short-term forecasting, the effect of the cyclical component is often assumed to be the same as included in recent time series values. However, for longer periods, or even for short periods during economic instability, the identification of the *cyclical turning points* for the national economy is important.

Remember

The cyclical variations associated with a particular product may or may not coincide with the general business cycle.

The National Bureau of Economic Research has identified a number of published time series that historically have been indicators of cyclic revivals and recessions with respect to the general business cycle. One group, called *leading indicators*, has usually reached cyclical turning points prior to the corresponding change in general economic activity. A second group, called *coincident indicators*, are time series that have generally had turning points coinciding with the general business cycle. The third group, called *lagging indicators*, are those time series for which the peaks and troughs usually lag behind those of the general business cycle.

Forecasting Based on Moving Averages

A *moving average* is the average of the most recent n data values in a time series. This procedure can be represented by:

$$MA = \frac{\Sigma(most\ recent\ n\ values)}{n}$$

As each new data value becomes available in a time series, the newest observation replaces the oldest observation in the set of n values as the basis for determining the new average, and this is why it is called a *moving* average.

The moving average can be used to forecast the data value for the next (forthcoming) period in the time series, but not for periods that are farther in the future. It is an appropriate method of forecasting when there is no trend, cyclical or seasonal influence on the data, which of course is an unlikely situation. The procedure serves simply to average out the irregular component in the recent time series data.

Exponential Smoothing as a Forecasting Method

Exponential smoothing is a method of forecasting that is also based on using a moving average, but it is a *weighted* moving average rather than one in which the preceding data values are equally weighted. The basis for the weights is exponential because the greatest weight is given to the data value for the pe-

riod immediately preceding the forecast period and the weights decrease exponentially for the data values of earlier periods. The method presented here is called *simple exponential smoothing*.

The following algebraic model serves to represent how the exponentially decreasing weights are determined. Specifically, where α is a smoothing constant discussed below, the most recent value of the time series is weighted by α, the next most recent value is weighted by $\alpha(1 - \alpha)$, the next value by $\alpha(1 - \alpha)^2$, and so forth, and all the weighted values are then summed to determine the forecast:

$$\hat{Y}_{t-1} = \alpha Y_t + \alpha(1-\alpha)Y_{t-1} + \alpha(1-\alpha)^2 Y_{t-2} + \cdots + \alpha(1-\alpha)^k Y_{t-k}$$

where:
$\hat{Y}_{t+1}$ = forecast for the next period
α = smoothing constant $(0 \leq \alpha \leq 1)$
Y_t = actual value for the most recent period
Y_{t-1} = actual value for the period preceding the most recent period
Y_{t-k} = actual value for k periods preceding the most recent period

Although the above formula serves to present the rationale of exponential smoothing, its use is quite cumbersome. A simplified procedure that requires an initial "seed" forecast but does not require the determination of weights is generally used instead. The formula for determining the forecast by the simplified method of exponential smoothing is:

$$\hat{Y}_{t+1} = \hat{Y}_t + \alpha(Y_t - \hat{Y}_t)$$

where:
$\hat{Y}_{t+1}$ = forecast for the next period
$\hat{Y}_t$ = forecast for the most recent period

α = smoothing constant $(0 \leq \alpha \leq 1)$
Y_t = actual value for the most recent period

Because the most recent time series value must be available to determine a forecast for the following period, simple exponential smoothing can be used only to forecast the value for the *next* period in the time series, not for several periods into the future. The closer the value of the smoothing constant is set to 1.0, the more heavily is the forecast weighted by the most recent results.

Other Forecasting Methods That Incorporate Smoothing

Whereas the moving average is appropriate as the basis for forecasting only when the irregular influence causes the time series values to vary, simple exponential smoothing is most appropriate only when the cyclical and irregular influences comprise the main effects on the observed values. In both methods, a forecast can be obtained only for the next period in the time series, and not for periods farther into the future. Other more complex methods of smoothing incorporate more influences and permit forecasting for several periods into the future. These methods are briefly described below. Full explanations and descriptions of these methods are included in specialized textbooks in forecasting.

Linear exponential smoothing utilizes a linear trend equation based on the time series data. However, unlike the simple trend equation presented earlier in this book, the values in the series are exponentially weighted based on the use of a smoothing constant. As in simple exponential smoothing, the constant can vary from 0 to 1.0.

Holt's exponential smoothing utilizes a linear trend equation based on using two smoothing constants: one to estimate the current level of the time series values and the other to estimate the slope.

Winter's exponential smoothing incorporates seasonal influences in the forecast. Three smoothing constants are used: one to estimate the current level of the time series values, the second to estimate the slope of the trend line, and the third to estimate the seasonal forecast to be used as a multiplier.

Autoregressive integrated moving average (ARIMA) *models* are a category of forecasting methods in which previously observed values in the time series are used as independent variables in regression models. The most widely used method in this category was developed by Box and Jenkins, and is generally called the *Box-Jenkins method*. These methods make explicit use of the existence of *autocorrelation* in the time series, which is the correlation between a variable, lagged one or more periods, with itself. The *Durbin-Watson test* serves to detect the existence of autocorrelated residuals (*serial correlation*) in time series values. A value of the test statistic close to 2.0 supports the null hypothesis that no autocorrelation exists in the time series. A value below 1.4 generally is indicative of strong positive serial correlation, while a value greater than 2.6 indicates the existence of strong negative serial correlation.

Solved Problems

Solved Problem 16.1 Table 16.1 presents sales data for an 11-year period for a software company incorporated in 1990. Included also are worktable calculations needed to determine the equation for the trend line. De-

Year	Coded year (X)	Sales, in millions (Y)	XY	X^2
1990	0	$ 0.2	0	0
1991	1	0.4	0.4	1
1992	2	0.5	1.0	4
1993	3	0.9	2.7	9
1994	4	1.1	4.4	16
1995	5	1.5	7.5	25
1996	6	1.3	7.8	36
1997	7	1.1	7.7	49
1998	8	1.7	13.6	64
1999	9	1.9	17.1	81
2000	10	2.3	23.0	100
Total	55	12.9	85.2	385

Table 16.1 Annual sales for a graphics software firm, with worktable to determine the equation for the trend line

termine the linear trend equation for these data by the least-square method, coding 1990 as 0 and carrying all values to two places beyond the decimal point. Using the equation determine the forecast of sales for the year 2001.

Solution: $Y_T = b_0 + b_1 X$
$X = 5.00$, $Y = 1.17$, $b_1 = 0.19$, and $b_0 = 0.22$
$Y_T = 0.22 + 0.19X$ (with $X = 0$ at 1990)
$Y_T(2001) = 0.22 + 0.19(11) = \$2.31$ (in millions)

This equation can be used as a beginning point for forecasting. The slope of 0.19 indicates that during the 11-year existence of the company there has been an average increase in sales of 0.19 million dollars annually. ($190,000)

Solved Problem 16.2 Refer to the annual time series data in Table 16.1. Using the actual level of sales for 1994 of 1.1 million dollars as the "seed" forecast for 1995, determine the forecast for each annual sales amount by the method of simple exponential smoothing. First use a smoothing constant of $\alpha = 0.80$, then use a smoothing constant of $\alpha = 0.20$, and compare the two sets of forecasts.

Solution: Table 16.2 is the worktable that reports the two sets of forecasts.

Year (t)	Sales in millions (Y_t)	$\alpha = 0.20$		$\alpha = 0.80$	
		Forecast $(\hat{Y}_t)$	Forecast error $(Y_t - \hat{Y}_t)$	Forecast $(\hat{Y}_t)$	Forecast error $(Y_t - \hat{Y}_t)$
1995	$1.5	$1.1	$0.4	$1.1	$0.4
1996	1.3	1.2	0.1	1.4	−0.1
1997	1.1	1.2	−0.1	1.3	−0.2
1998	1.7	1.2	0.5	1.1	0.6
1999	1.9	1.3	0.6	1.6	0.3
2000	2.3	1.4	0.9	1.8	0.5
2001		1.6		2.2	

Table 16.2 Year-by-Year forecasts by the method of exponential smoothing

The forecast errors are generally lower for $\alpha = 0.80$. Thus, the greater weight given to the forecast errors leads to better forecasts for these data.

Chapter 17
DECISION ANALYSIS: PAYOFF TABLES AND DECISION TREES

IN THIS CHAPTER:

✔ *The Structure of Payoff Tables*
✔ *Decision Making Based upon Probabilities Alone*
✔ *Decision Making Based upon Economic Consequences Alone*
✔ *Decision Making Based upon Both Probabilities and Economic Consequences: The Expected Payoff Criterion*
✔ *Expected Utility as the Decision Criterion*
✔ *Solved Problems*

The Structure of Payoff Tables

From the standpoint of statistical decision theory, a decision situation under conditions of uncertainty can be represented by certain common ingredients that are included in the structure of the *payoff table* for the situation. Essentially, a payoff table identifies the conditional gain (or loss) associated with every possible combination of decision acts and events; it also typically indicates the probability of occurrence for each of the mutually exclusive events.

In Table 17.1, the *acts* are the alternative courses of action, or strategies, that are available to the decision maker. As the result of the analysis, one of these acts is chosen as being the best act. The basis for this choice is the subject matter of this chapter. As a minimum, there must be at least two possible acts available, so that the opportunity for choice in fact exists.

Events	Probability	Acts				
		A_1	A_2	A_3	...	A_n
E_1	P_1	X_{11}	X_{12}	X_{13}	...	X_{1n}
E_2	P_2	X_{21}	X_{22}	X_{23}	...	X_{2n}
E_3	P_3	X_{31}	X_{32}	X_{33}	...	X_{3n}
...	...	...	...	...	...	...
E_m	P_m	X_{m1}	X_{m2}	X_{m3}	...	X_{mn}

Table 17.1 General structure of a payoff table

The *events* identify the occurrences that are outside of the decision maker's control and that determine the level of success for a given act. These events are often called "states of nature," "states," or "outcomes." We are concerned only with discrete events in this chapter.

The *probability* of each event is included as part of the general format of a decision table when such probability values are in fact available. However, one characteristic of decision analysis is that such probabilities should always be available since they can be based on either objective data or be determined subjectively on the basis of judgment.

Note!

Because the events in the payoff table are mutually exclusive and exhaustive, the sum of the probability values should be 1.0.

Finally, the cell entries are the conditional values, or conditional economic consequences. These values are usually called *payoffs* in the literature, and they are conditional in the sense that the economic result that is experienced depends on the decision act that is chosen and the event that occurs.

Decision Making Based upon Probabilities Alone

In such cases, one decision criterion that might be used is to identify the event with the *maximum probability* of occurrence and to choose the decision act corresponding with that event. Another basis for choosing the best act would be to calculate the *expectation* of the event and to choose the act accordingly. However, because neither of these criteria make reference to the economic consequences associated with the various decisions acts and events, they represent an incomplete basis for choosing the best decision.

Decision Making Based upon Economic Consequences Alone

The payoff matrix that is used in conjunction with decision making based only upon economic consequences is similar to Table 17.1, except for the absence of the probability distribution associated with the possible events. Three criteria that have been described and used in conjunction with such a decision matrix are the maximin, maximax, and minimax regret criteria.

The *maximin criterion* is the standard by which the best act is the one for which the minimum value is larger than the minimum for any other decision act. Use of this criterion leads to a highly conservative decision strategy, in that the decision maker is particularly concerned about the "worst that can happen" with respect to each act. Computationally, the minimum value in each column of the payoff table is determined, and the best act is the one for which the resulting value is largest.

The *maximax criterion* is the standard by which the best act is the one for which the maximum value is larger than the maximum for any other decision act. This criterion is philosophically the opposite of the maximin criterion, since the decision maker is particularly oriented toward the "best that can happen" with respect to each act. Computationally, the maximum value in each column of the payoff table is determined, and the best act is the one for which the resulting value is largest.

Analysis by the *minimax regret* criterion is based on so-called regrets rather than on conditional values as such. A *regret*, or conditional *opportunity loss*, for each act is the difference between the economic outcome for the act and the economic outcome of the best act *given that a particular event has occurred*. Thus, the best or most desirable regret value is "0," which indicates that the act perfectly matched with the given event. Also, note that even when there is an economic gain associated with a particular act and a given event, there could also be an opportunity loss, because some other act could result in a higher payoff with the given event.

Decision Making Based upon Both Probabilities and Economic Consequences: The Expected Payoff Criterion

The methods presented in this section utilize all the information contained in the basic payoff table. Thus, we consider both the probabilities associated with the possible events and the economic consequences for all combinations of the several acts and several events.

The *expected payoff* (EP) criterion is the standard by which the best act is the one for which the expected economic outcome is the highest, as a long-run average. Note that in the present case we are concerned about the long-run average economic result, and not simply the long-run average event value (demand level) discussed earlier.

You Need to Know

Computationally, the expected payoff for each act is determined by multiplying the conditional payoff for each event/act combination by the probability of the event and summing these products for each act.

The best act identified by the expected payoff criterion can also be determined by identifying the act with the minimum expected opportunity loss (*EOL*) or expected regret. This is so because the act with the largest expected gain logically would have the smallest expected regret.

Expected Utility as the Decision Criterion

The expected payoff criterion is typically used in conjunction with both payoff table analysis and decision tree analysis. However, when the decision maker perceives one or more of the economic consequences as being unusually large or small, the expected payoff criterion does not necessarily provide the basis for identifying the "best" decision. This is particularly likely for unique, rather than repetitive, situations.

Utility is a measure of value that expresses the true relative value of various outcomes, including economic consequences, for a decision maker. Any given utility scale can begin at an arbitrary minimum value and have an arbitrarily assigned maximum value. However, it is convenient to have utility values begin at a minimum of 0 and extend to a maximum of 1.00, and this is the scale most frequently used. With such a scale, an outcome with a utility of 0.60 is understood to be twice as desirable as one with a utility of 0.30.

Using a *reference contract*, you can determine an individual's utility values for different monetary values. By this approach, the individual is asked to designate an *amount certain* that would be accepted, or paid, as being equivalent to each of a series of uncertain situations involving risk. The first risk situation portrayed always includes the two extreme limits of the range of monetary values of interest.

Solved Problems

Solved Problem 17.1 Based on a new technological approach, a manufacturer has developed a color TV set with a 45-in. picture tube. The owner of a small retail store estimates that at the selling price of $2,800 the probability values associated with selling 2, 3, 4, or 5 sets during the three months of concern are 0.30, 0.40, 0.20 and 0.10, respectively. Based only on these probability values, how many sets should the retailer order for stock, assuming no reorders are possible during the period?

Solution: Based on the criterion of maximum probability, three sets should be ordered, since the probability 0.40 associated with three sets being sold is higher than the probability of any other event. On the other hand, the expectation of the demand level is 3.1. Based on this expectation of the event, the act that comes closest to corresponding with it is also that of ordering three sets.

	Order quantity			
Market demand	A_1: 2	A_2: 3	A_3: 4	A_4: 5
E_1: 2	$400	$100	− $200	− $ 500
E_2: 3	400	600	300	0
E_3: 4	400	600	800	500
E_4: 5	400	600	800	1,000
Minimum	$400	$100	− $200	− $ 500
Maximum	$400	$600	$800	$1,000

Table 17.2 Number of TV sets to be ordered according to the maximin and maximax criteria

CHAPTER 17: Decision Analysis **161**

Solved Problem 17.2 For the inventory decision situation in Solved Problem 17.1, the profit margin for each set sold is $200. If any sets are not sold during the three months, the total loss per set to the retailer will be $300. Based on these economic consequences alone, and ignoring the probability values identified in Solved Problem 17.1, determine the best decision act from the standpoint of the maximin and the maximax criteria.

Solution: With reference to Table 17.2, for the maximin criterion the best act is A_1: Order two sets. For the maximax criterion, the best act is A_4: Order five sets.

Chapter 18
STATISTICAL PROCESS CONTROL

IN THIS CHAPTER:

- ✔ *Total Quality Management*
- ✔ *Statistical Quality Control*
- ✔ *Types of Variation in Processes*
- ✔ *Control Charts*
- ✔ *Solved Problems*

Total Quality Management

Total Quality Management (TQM) is an approach to management in which the quality of the organization's output is given first and foremost attention. The output can be in the form either of a product or service. Further, the output may be one that is delivered to external customers, or it may be internal output to other units of the organization. How is quality determined? It is based on the judgment of the customer. Thus, customer satisfaction is the ultimate objective of TQM.

The TQM approach not only sets out to achieve high quality, but incorporates the philosophy by which this objective can be achieved. Traditional methods of quality assurance focused on finding and correcting product defects. The result was the use of a hierarchical command structure and an ever-increasing number of inspection steps. In an inspection-oriented manufacturing plant, half of the workers can be involved in finding and reworking rejects. The TQM philosophy is that quality should be *designed into the product or service*, and that sampling-based statistical quality control should be used, rather than attempting to inspect every unit of output. Further, quality should be monitored by those who are responsible for the output, rather than by staff personnel who represent higher management echelons. This approach results in elimination of traditional inspectors. Instead, employee teams have both the authority and responsibility for the quality of their output and its improvement. Thus, employee participation in setting unit goals and devising the strategies by which they are to be achieved is critical to the success of TQM.

 **Note!**

An example of an external product output is the production of video recorders. An example of an internal product output is the production of the gear department being sent to the transmission assembly department of a vehicle plant.

Statistical Quality Control

Although there are several different ingredients that constitute TQM, the statistical contribution has its roots in statistical quality control. Sampling techniques for quality inspection date back to the 1930s. These include the development of statistically-based sampling plans as an alternative to 100 percent inspection and the associated use of control charts. However it was not until the 1970s, when U.S. industry began to react seriously to the high quality of products imported from Japan, that the application of statistical quality control became widespread. The continuing trade imbalance with Japan became a national issue during the 1980s and 1990s, and thus spurred further interest in quality improvement

Ironically, the high quality of Japanese products was achieved largely because they adopted suggestions of U.S. consultants in the restructuring of their manufacturing processes after World War II. Preeminent among these consultants was the statistician W. Edwards Deming, after whom the Deming Award for Quality was named in Japan. Deming developed a philosophy of quality management that was the precursor of what is now called Total Quality Management, and which he summarized in his "14 Points."

1. Create consistency of purpose for improvement of products and services. That purpose should be quality, not short-term profits.

2. Adopt the new philosophy. Reject the focus on the inspection-rejection-rework viewpoint in favor of a preventive approach.

3. Cease dependence on mass inspection to achieve quality. Improve product design and institute sampling-based process control.

4. End the practice of awarding business on the basis of price tag alone. Consider quality and the development of supplier loyalty.

5. Improve constantly and forever the system of production and service.

6. Institute training.

7. Institute leadership. Autocratic management is not true leadership.

8. Drive out fear. People do their best work if they feel secure.

9. Break down barriers between departments. Different areas should not have conflicting goals.

10. Eliminate slogans, exhortations, and numerical targets for the work force. Simply telling people to improve does not work.

11. Eliminate numerical quotas. Such quotas do not take quality into consideration, and in centralized economies such quotas have often been achieved at the expense of other products or services.

12. Remove barriers to pride of workmanship. These include poor supervision, poor product design, defective materials, and defective machines.

13. Institute a vigorous program of education and self-improvement for everyone in the organization. This includes the need to know modern methods of statistical process control.

14. Take action to accomplish the transformation. This requires the leadership of top management to establish the new environment.

Table 18.1 Deming's 14 Points

Types of Variation in Processes

A *process* is a sequence of operations by which such inputs as labor, materials, and methods are transformed into outputs, in the form of products or services. Earlier in the chapter we differentiated internal and external outputs as well as product and service outputs. In any process, some *variation* in the quality measure from product to product or from service to service is unavoidable.

Statistical process control refers to the application of the methods of statistical quality control to the monitoring of processes (and not just to the inspection of the final outputs of the processes). The purpose is to control the quality of product or service outputs from a process by maintaining control of the process. When a process is described as being "in control," it means that the amount of variation in the output is relatively constant and within established limits that are deemed acceptable. There are two kinds of causes of variation in a process. *Common causes* of variation to be expected. *Assignable causes,* or *special causes*, of variation due to unusual factors that are not part of the process design and not ordinarily part of the process.

A *stable process* is one in which only common causes of variation affect the output quality. Such a process can also be described as being in a state of *statistical control*. An *unstable process* is one in which both assignable causes and common causes affect the output quality. Such a process can also be described as being *out of control*, particularly when the assignable cause is controllable.

The way we set out to improve the quality of output for a process depends on the source of process variation. *For a process that is stable*, improvement can take place only by improving the design of the process. A pervasive error in process management is *tampering*, which is to take actions that presume that a process is not in control, when in fact it is stable. Such actions only increase variability, and are analogous to the overcorrecting that new drivers do in learning to steer a car. For a process that is unstable, improvement can be achieved by identifying and correcting the assignable causes.

Control Charts

A *control chart* is a time series plot with levels of output quality on the vertical axis and a sequence of time periods on the horizontal axis. For statistical process control the measurements that are graphed are sample data collected by the *method of rational subgroups* as described in the section on Other Sampling Methods in Chapter 1. The chart includes *lower and upper control limits* that identify the range of variation that can be ascribed to common causes. The standard practice is to place the control limits at three standard error units above and below the target quality level; this is called the *3-sigma rule*. Two types of control charts that are used to monitor the level of process quality are control charts for the *mean* and for the *proportion*. Two types of control charts that are used to monitor process variability are control charts for the *range* and for the *standard deviation*.

Solved Problems

Solved Problem 18.1 From the perspective of TQM, who ultimately determines the quality of a product or service?

Solution: The customer of that product or service.

Solved Problem 18.2 Who has the responsibility for quality control in a traditional manufacturing plant, as contrasted to a plant that follows the TQM philosophy?

Solution: By the traditional approach, inspectors are employees of a quality control staff that, in effect, represents upper management control of operations. In contrast, TQM places full authority and responsibility for quality on the employee groups and their supervisors who produce the output.

Solved Problem 18.3 Differentiate a stable process from an unstable process.

Solution: A stable process is one that exhibits only common cause variation. An unstable process exhibits variation due to both assignable and common causes.

Solved Problem 18.4 Describe how the output of a stable process can be improved. What actions do not improve a stable process, but rather, make the output more variable?

Solution: A stable process can be improved only by changing the design of the process. Attempts to make adjustments to a stable process, which is called tampering, results in more variation in the quality of the output.

Solved Problem 18.5 What is the purpose of maintaining control charts?

Solution: Control charts are used to detect the occurrence of assignable causes affecting the quality of process output.

Appendix A

Proportions of Area for the Standard Normal Distribution

Areas reported below:*

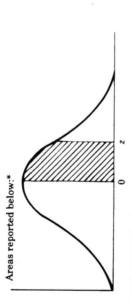

z	.00	.01	.02	.03	.04	.05	.06	.07	.08	.09
0.0	.0000	.0040	.0080	.0120	.0160	.0199	.0239	.0279	.0319	.0359
0.1	.0398	.0438	.0478	.0517	.0557	.0596	.0636	.0675	.0714	.0753
0.2	.0793	.0832	.0871	.0910	.0948	.0987	.1026	.1064	.1103	.1141
0.3	.1179	.1217	.1255	.1293	.1331	.1368	.1406	.1443	.1480	.1517
0.4	.1554	.1591	.1628	.1664	.1700	.1736	.1772	.1808	.1844	.1879
0.5	.1915	.1950	.1985	.2019	.2054	.2088	.2123	.2157	.2190	.2224
0.6	.2257	.2291	.2324	.2357	.2389	.2422	.2454	.2486	.2518	.2549
0.7	.2580	.2612	.2642	.2673	.2704	.2734	.2764	.2794	.2823	.2852
0.8	.2881	.2910	.2939	.2967	.2995	.3023	.3051	.3078	.3106	.3133
0.9	.3159	.3186	.3212	.3238	.3264	.3289	.3315	.3340	.3365	.3389

z	.00	.01	.02	.03	.04	.05	.06	.07	.08	.09
1.0	.3413	.3438	.3461	.3485	.3508	.3531	.3554	.3577	.3599	.3621
1.1	.3643	.3665	.3686	.3708	.3729	.3749	.3770	.3790	.3810	.3830
1.2	.3849	.3869	.3888	.3907	.3925	.3944	.3962	.3980	.3997	.4014
1.3	.4032	.4049	.4066	.4082	.4099	.4115	.4131	.4147	.4162	.4177
1.4	.4192	.4207	.4222	.4236	.4251	.4265	.4279	.4292	.4306	.4319
1.5	.4332	.4345	.4357	.4370	.4382	.4394	.4406	.4418	.4429	.4441
1.6	.4452	.4463	.4474	.4484	.4495	.4505	.4515	.4525	.4535	.4545
1.7	.4554	.4564	.4573	.4582	.4591	.4599	.4608	.4616	.4625	.4633
1.8	.4641	.4649	.4656	.4664	.4671	.4678	.4686	.4693	.4699	.4706
1.9	.4713	.4719	.4725	.4732	.4738	.4744	.4750	.4756	.4761	.4767
2.0	.4772	.4778	.4783	.4788	.4793	.4798	.4803	.4808	.4812	.4817
2.1	.4821	.4826	.4830	.4834	.4838	.4842	.4846	.4850	.4854	.4857
2.2	.4861	.4864	.4868	.4871	.4875	.4878	.4881	.4884	.4887	.4890
2.3	.4893	.4896	.4898	.4901	.4904	.4906	.4909	.4911	.4913	.4916
2.4	.4918	.4920	.4922	.4925	.4927	.4929	.4931	.4932	.4934	.4936
2.5	.4938	.4940	.4941	.4943	.4945	.4946	.4948	.4949	.4951	.4952
2.6	.4953	.4955	.4956	.4957	.4959	.4960	.4961	.4962	.4963	.4964
2.7	.4965	.4966	.4967	.4968	.4969	.4970	.4971	.4972	.4973	.4974
2.8	.4974	.4975	.4976	.4977	.4977	.4978	.4979	.4979	.4980	.4981
2.9	.4981	.4982	.4983	.4983	.4984	.4984	.4985	.4985	.4986	.4986
3.0	.4987									
3.5	.4997									
4.0	.4999									

* Example: for z = 1.96, shaded area is 0.4750 out of the total area of 1.0000

169

Appendix B

Proportions of Area for the *t* Distribution

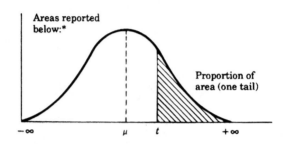

Areas reported below:*

Proportion of area (one tail)

$-\infty$ μ t $+\infty$

df	0.10	0.05	0.025	0.01	0.005	df	0.10	0.05	0.025	0.01	0.005
1	3.078	6.314	12.706	31.821	63.657	18	1.330	1.734	2.101	2.552	2.878
2	1.886	2.920	4.303	6.965	9.925	19	1.328	1.729	2.093	2.539	2.861
3	1.638	2.353	3.182	4.541	5.841	20	1.325	1.725	2.086	2.528	2.845
4	1.533	2.132	2.776	3.747	4.604	21	1.323	1.721	2.080	2.518	2.831
5	1.476	2.015	2.571	3.365	4.032	22	1.321	1.717	2.074	2.508	2.819
6	1.440	1.943	2.447	3.143	3.707	23	1.319	1.714	2.069	2.500	2.807
7	1.415	1.895	2.365	2.998	3.499	24	1.318	1.711	2.064	2.492	2.797
8	1.397	1.860	2.306	2.896	2.355	25	1.316	1.708	2.060	2.485	2.787
9	1.383	1.833	2.262	2.821	3.250						
10	1.372	1.812	2.228	2.764	3.169	26	1.315	1.706	2.056	2.479	2.779
						27	1.314	1.703	2.052	2.473	2.771
11	1.363	1.796	2.201	2.718	3.106	28	1.313	1.701	2.048	2.467	2.763
12	1.356	1.782	2.179	2.681	3.055	29	1.311	1.699	2.045	2.462	2.756
13	1.350	1.771	2.160	2.650	3.012	30	1.310	1.697	2.042	2.457	2.750
14	1.345	1.761	2.145	2.624	2.977						
15	1.341	1.753	2.131	2.602	2.947	40	1.303	1.684	2.021	2.423	2.704
						60	1.296	1.671	2.000	2.390	2.660
16	1.337	1.746	2.120	2.583	2.921	120	1.289	1.658	1.980	2.358	2.617
17	1.333	1.740	2.110	2.567	2.898	∞	1.282	1.645	1.960	2.326	2.576

* Example: For the shaded area to represent 0.05 of the total area of 1.0, value of *t* with 10 degrees of freedom is 1.812.

170

Appendix C

Proportions of Area for the χ^2 Distribution

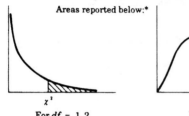

Areas reported below:*

For $df = 1,2$ For $df \geq 3$

df	Proportion of area					
	0.500	0.100	0.050	0.025	0.010	0.005
1	0.455	2.71	3.84	5.02	6.63	7.88
2	1.386	4.61	5.99	7.38	9.21	10.60
3	2.366	6.25	7.81	9.35	11.34	12.84
4	3.357	7.78	9.49	11.14	13.28	14.86
5	4.251	9.24	11.07	12.83	15.09	16.75
6	5.35	10.64	12.59	14.45	16.81	18.55
7	6.35	12.02	14.07	16.01	18.48	20.28
8	7.34	13.36	15.51	17.53	20.09	21.96
9	8.34	14.68	16.92	19.02	21.67	23.59
10	9.34	15.99	18.31	20.48	23.21	25.19
11	10.34	17.28	19.68	21.92	24.73	26.76
12	11.34	18.55	21.03	23.34	26.22	28.30
13	12.34	19.81	22.36	24.74	27.69	29.82
14	13.34	21.06	23.68	26.12	29.14	31.32
15	14.34	22.31	25.00	27.49	30.58	32.80
16	15.34	23.54	26.30	28.85	32.00	34.27
17	16.34	24.77	27.59	30.19	33.41	35.72
18	17.34	25.99	28.87	31.53	34.81	37.16
19	18.34	27.20	30.14	32.85	36.19	38.58
20	19.34	28.41	31.41	34.17	37.57	40.00
21	20.34	29.62	32.67	35.48	38.93	41.40
22	21.34	30.81	33.92	36.78	40.29	42.80
23	22.34	32.01	35.17	38.08	41.64	44.18
24	23.34	33.20	36.42	39.36	42.98	45.56
25	24.34	34.38	37.65	40.65	44.31	46.93
26	25.34	35.56	38.89	41.92	45.64	48.29
27	26.34	36.74	40.11	43.19	46.96	49.64
28	27.34	37.92	41.34	44.46	48.28	50.99
29	28.34	39.09	42.56	45.72	49.59	52.34
30	29.34	40.26	43.77	46.98	50.89	53.67

*Example: For the shaded area to represent 0.05 of the total area of 1.0 under the density function, the value of χ^2 is 18.31 when $df = 10$.

Appendix D

Values of *F* Exceeded with Probabilities of 5 and 1%

		df (numerator)								
	1	2	3	4	5	6	7	8	9	10
1	161	200	216	225	230	234	237	239	241	242
	4,052	4,999	5,403	5,625	5,764	5,859	5,928	5,981	6,022	6,056
2	18 51	19 00	19 16	19 25	19 30	19 33	19 36	19 37	19 38	19 39
	98.49	99.00	99.17	99.25	99.30	99.33	99.36	99.37	99 39	99.40
3	10 13	9 55	9 28	9 12	9 01	8 94	8 88	8 84	8 81	8 78
	34.12	30.82	29.46	28.71	28.24	27.91	27.67	27.49	27.34	27.23
4	7 71	6 94	6 59	6 39	6 26	6 16	6 09	6 04	6 00	5 96
	21.20	18.00	16.69	15.98	15.52	15.21	14.98	14.80	14.66	14.54
5	6 61	5 79	5 41	5 19	5 05	4 95	4 88	4 82	4 78	4 74
	16.26	13.27	12.06	11.39	10.97	10.67	10.45	10.29	10.15	10.05
6	5 99	5 14	4 76	4 53	4 39	4 28	4 21	4 15	4 10	4 06
	13.74	10.92	9.78	9.15	8.75	8.47	8.26	8.10	7.98	7.87
7	5 59	4 74	4 34	4 12	3 97	3 87	3 79	3 73	3 68	3 63
	12.25	9.55	8.45	7.85	7.46	7.19	7.00	6.84	6.71	6.62
8	5 32	4 46	4 07	3 84	3 69	3 58	3 50	3 44	3 39	3 34
	11.26	8.65	7.59	7.01	6.63	6.37	6.19	6.03	5.91	5.82
9	5 12	4 26	3 86	3 63	3 48	3 37	3 29	3 23	3 18	3 13
	10.56	8.02	6.99	6.42	6.06	5.80	5.62	5.47	5.35	5.26
10	4 96	4 10	3 71	3 48	3 33	3 22	3 14	3 07	3 02	2 97
	10.04	7.56	6.55	5.99	5.64	5.39	5.21	5.06	4.95	4.85

df (denominator)

Index